Dürrenmatt

A STUDY OF HIS PLAYS

by

URS JENNY

translated by Keith Hamnett and Hugh Rorrison
with additional material by K. S. Whitton

EYRE METHUEN LTD
11 NEW FETTER LANE LONDON EC4P 4EE

Note: Quotations from Dürrenmatt's plays and other writings are taken from the published English translations where these exist (see Bibliography). In the case of *Portrait of a Planet* and *The Conformer*, James Kirkup's authorised but unpublished translations were used and thanks are due to Mr Kirkup and his agent, Michael Imison of Dr Jan Van Loewen Ltd, for making these available. In all other cases the translation is the work of Keith Hamnett and/or Hugh Rorrison.

Originally published in German as Dürrenmatt
*in 1965, and published in revised editions
in 1968 and 1973 by Friedrich Verlag*
© *1965, 1968 and 1973 Friedrich Verlag
Velber bei Hannover*

*First published in Great Britain in 1978
by Eyre Methuen Ltd
11 New Fetter Lane London EC4P 4EE
This translation* © *1978 Eyre Methuen Ltd*

ISBN 0 413 29050 6 hardback
ISBN 0 413 29060 3 paperback

Dürrenmatt

In the same series

Contents

Friedrich Dürrenmatt

1921 5th January: Friedrich Dürrenmatt born in Konol-
      fingen, Canton Bern, Switzerland. His father: Rein-
      hold Dürrenmatt, Protestant minister. His grandfather:
      Ulrich Dürrenmatt, politician, Member of Parliament,
      well known as a satirical poet.

1933–1935 Attends secondary school in the neighbouring
      village of Grosshöchstetten.

1935 Family moves to Bern, where his father becomes
      chaplain at the Salemspital. Dürrenmatt attends the
      Freies Gymnasium for two years then the Humboldt-
      ianum until he matriculates.

1941 Begins studying literature and philosophy at Univer-
      sity, first in Zurich for a semester only, then in Bern.
      Paints and draws a good deal. Reads Aristophanes,
      Kierkegaard, Heym, Trakl and, later, Kafka.

1943 First attempts at writing: the unpublished, unper-
      formed play, COMEDY (*Komödie*): 'Monstrous fan-
      tasies of Hell with whores, drunks, technicians, muti-
      lated people' (Hans Bänziger); and the prose pieces,
      CHRISTMAS (*Weihnachten*) and THE TORTURER (*Der
      Folterknecht*).
      'Up till then, being adept at drawing, I had only felt
      truly at home in the visual medium, which constituted
      a not inconsiderable risk for me. So I tried to study
      philosophy – a strange way out perhaps, but there was
      no other way open by which I could create a distance
      between myself and the visual images which possessed
      me, however slight that distance might have been at

first, a distance which would allow me to breathe at least a little. It was almost a matter of conquering a magnetism that was much too strong' (Dürrenmatt in 1952).

1945   First publication: the short story THE OLD MAN (*Der Alte*) appears in the Bern daily paper *Der Bund*.

Writes the prose pieces, THE PICTURE OF SISYPHUS (*Das Bild des Sisyphos*) and THE THEATRE MANAGER (*Der Theaterdirektor*), and starts work on IT IS WRITTEN (*Es steht geschrieben*).

1946   Completes IT IS WRITTEN. Writes the prose pieces, THE TRAP (*Die Falle*) and PILATE (*Pilatus*), and the radio play, THE DOPPELGANGER (*Der Doppelgänger*).

1947   Marries Lotti Geissler.

19th April: World première of IT IS WRITTEN at Zurich Schauspielhaus (director: Kurt Horwitz; designer: Teo Otto; with Gustav Knuth (Bockelson) and Heinrich Gretler (Knipperdollinck)). 'The première was a riot . . . Dürrenmatt's debut was greeted with so much whistling and booing that the police could not cope. The actors, however, showed remarkable sang-froid and the play was able to carry on to the end and to applause that sounded convinced' (Elisabeth Brock-Sulzer). The text of the play is published with six line-drawings by Dürrenmatt.

Works on THE BLIND DUKE (*Der Blinde*), and on a novel, eventually published as the fragment, THE CITY (*Die Stadt*) in 1952.

1948   10th January: World première of THE BLIND DUKE at Basle Stadttheater (director: Ernst Ginsberg; with Kurt Horwitz in the title role).

Works on ROMULUS THE GREAT (*Romulus der Grosse*), and writes several sketches for the Cabaret Cornichon in Zurich, two of which are performed.

Moves house to Ligerz on the Bielersee.

Writes four acts of a play called THE TOWER OF BABEL (*Der Turmbau von Babel*) which he then abandons and destroys.

1949   25th April: World première of ROMULUS THE GREAT at Basle Stadttheater (director: Ernst Ginsberg; with Kurt Horwitz in the title role).

October: Première of first Dürrenmatt play to be performed in Germany, ROMULUS THE GREAT in Göttingen.

1950   Writes the detective story, THE JUDGE AND HIS HANGMAN (*Der Richter und sein Henker*) in serial form for the magazine *Der Schweizerische Beobachter*. Starts work on THE MARRIAGE OF MR MISSISSIPPI (*Die Ehe des Herrn Mississippi*).

1951   Writes second serial novel, THE QUARRY (*Der Verdacht*), the radio play, THE CASE OF THE DONKEY'S SHADOW (*Der Prozess um des Esels Schatten*), and the prose piece, THE DOG (*Der Hund*).

Contributes theatre criticism to the Zurich 'Weltwoche' (reprinted in *Theater-Schriften und Reden*).

1952   Buys a house in Neuchâtel.

26th March: World première of THE MARRIAGE OF MR MISSISSIPPI at Munich Kammerspiele (see page 171).

Writes the prose pieces, THE TUNNEL (*Der Tunnel*) and the unpublished MR X TAKES A HOLIDAY (*Mister X macht Ferien*), and the radio plays, STRANITZKY AND THE NATIONAL HERO (*Stranitzky und der Nationalheld*) and CONVERSATION AT NIGHT (*Nächtliches Gespräch mit einem verachteten Menschen*), which is first performed on stage at Munich Kammerspiele on 26th July.

Publication of a book of nine short stories and prose pieces under the title THE CITY.

First foreign language production of a Dürrenmatt play, LES FOUS DE DIEU (IT IS WRITTEN) at Théâtre des Mathurins, Paris.

1953   22nd December: World première of AN ANGEL COMES TO BABYLON (*Ein Engel kommt nach Babylon*) at Munich Kammerspiele (director: Hans Schweikart; designer: Caspar Neher; with Erich Ponto (Akki) and Peter Lühr (Nebuchadnezzar)).

1954   Writes the radio plays, HERCULES AND THE AUGEAN STABLES (*Herkules und der Stall des Augias*) and OPERATION WEGA (*Das Unternehmen der Wega*), and the essay, PROBLEMS OF THE THEATRE (*Theaterprobleme*).

Directs a production of THE MARRIAGE OF MR MISSISSIPPI at Bern Stadttheater.

1955   Writes the novel, ONCE A GREEK (*Grieche sucht Griechin*), and the play, THE VISIT (*Der Besuch der alten Dame*).

1956   29th January: World première of THE VISIT at Zurich Schauspielhaus (see page 175).

Writes the radio plays, A DANGEROUS GAME (*Die Panne*), which is later rewritten as a short story, then adapted for television, and INCIDENT AT TWILIGHT (*Abendstunde im Spätherbst*), and a new version of THE MARRIAGE OF MR MISSISSIPPI.

October: Directs a production of THE VISIT in Basle.

1957   Writes television adaptation of THE JUDGE AND HIS HANGMAN, and screenplay for the film ASSAULT IN BROAD DAYLIGHT (*Es geschah am hellichten Tag*) (director: Ladislao Vajda), the material of which he redeveloped in the novel THE PLEDGE (*Das Versprechen*).

New versions of AN ANGEL COMES TO BABYLON and ROMULUS THE GREAT, which is produced at Zurich Schauspielhaus on 24th October.

Plans for collaboration with Max Frisch: Dürrenmatt intends writing a counter-play to *The Fire Raisers* with Knechtling as the main character, but the project falls through.

Publication of first volume of collected COMEDIES (*Komödien I*).

1958 Works with Paul Burkhard on FRANK V (*Frank der Fünfte*).

2nd April: New York première of FOOLS ARE PASSING THROUGH (adaptation by Maximilian Slater of *Die Ehe des Herrn Mississippi*) at Jan Hus Auditorium (director: Maximilian Slater).

5th May: New York première of THE VISIT (see page 177).

1959 19th March: World première of FRANK V at Zurich Schauspielhaus (director: Oskar Wälterlin; designer: Teo Otto; with Kurt Horwitz, Therese Giehse, Maria Becker, Ernst Schröder, Gustav Knuth).

24th September: ONE EVENING IN LATE AUTUMN (*Abendstunde im Spätherbst*) broadcast on BBC Home Service.

30th September: British première of THE MARRIAGE OF MR MISSISSIPPI at Arts Theatre, London (director: Clifford Williams; with Patricia Kneale, Douglas Wilmer).

9th November: Dürrenmatt gives the lecture FRIEDRICH SCHILLER on being presented with the Schiller Prize of the city of Mannheim.

19th November: stage adaptation of INCIDENT AT TWILIGHT produced at Renaissancetheater, Berlin.

December: Dürrenmatt directs a workshop-theatre version of THE VISIT at Ateliertheater, Bern.

1960 31st January: Italian première of THE VISIT in Milan (see page 178).

2nd February: New York première of THE DEADLY

GAME (adapted for the stage by James Yaffe from the short story *Die Panne*) at Longacre Theatre.

23rd March: New York première of THE JACKASS (adapted for the stage by George White from the radio play *Der Prozess um des Esels Schatten*) at Barbizon Plaza Theatre.

23rd June: British première of THE VISIT (New York production) at Royalty Theatre, London.

23rd August: Edinburgh Festival production of ROMULUS THE GREAT by Glasgow Citizens' Theatre Company at Gateway Theatre, Edinburgh (director: Callum Mill).

Dürrenmatt writes screenplay for film version of THE MARRIAGE OF MR MISSISSIPPI (director: Kurt Horwitz; with Hans Schweikart), and a new ending for the Munich production of FRANK V.

Works on a so far unpublished novel with the title JUSTICE (*Justiz*).

1961 Writes THE PHYSICISTS (*Die Physiker*).

Publication of COLLECTED RADIO PLAYS (*Gesammelte Hörspiele*) and of a third version of ROMULUS THE GREAT.

17th December: THE JUDGE AND HIS HANGMAN (adapted for television by Sheila Hodgson) televised by BBC–TV (producer: Peter Dews).

1962 10th January: New York première of ROMULUS (adapted by Gore Vidal from *Romulus der Grosse*) at Music Box Theatre (director: Joseph Anthony; with Cyril Ritchard).

20th February: World première of THE PHYSICISTS at Zurich Schauspielhaus (see page 182).

Rewrites the radio play, HERCULES AND THE AUGEAN STABLES as a stage play.

1963 9th January: British première of THE PHYSICISTS at Aldwych Theatre, London (see page 185).

20th March: World première of HERCULES AND THE AUGEAN STABLES at Zurich Schauspielhaus (director: Leonard Steckel; designer: Teo Otto; with Gustav Knuth and Ernst Schröder).

26th March: British première of AN ANGEL COMES TO BABYLON by Bristol Old Vic Company at Theatre Royal, Bristol (director: Val May).

8th April: British première of THE DEADLY GAME (Yaffe adaptation) at Ashcroft Theatre, Croydon (produced in London at Savoy Theatre on 26th April 1967).

Writes THE WEDDING OF HELVETIA AND MERCURY (*Die Hochzeit der Helvetia mit dem Merkur*), a theatrical cantata for the Swiss cabaret act, Voli Geiler and Walter Morath.

Produces a number of satirical drawings under the title THE HOMELAND IN POSTERS (*Die Heimat im Plakat*).

1964   Prepares a new version of FRANK V for a production in Bochum which does not take place.

Film of THE VISIT made for Twentieth Century-Fox without Dürrenmatt's co-operation (director: Bernhard Wicki; with Ingrid Bergman and Anthony Quinn).

Publication of second volume of collected COMEDIES AND EARLY PLAYS (*Komödien II und frühe Stücke*).

13th October: New York première of THE PHYSICISTS at Martin Beck Theatre (director: Peter Brook; with Jessica Tandy, Hume Cronyn, Robert Shaw, George Voskovec).

1965   Works on THE METEOR (*Der Meteor*), and on a so far unpublished prose work satirically depicting a secret session of the Kremlin.

1966   20th January: World première of THE METEOR at Zurich Schauspielhaus; produced in Germany on

9th February in Hamburg and on 12th February in Munich (see page 186).

March: British première of HERCULES AND THE AUGEAN STABLES at Questors Theatre, Ealing.

19th July: British première of CONVERSATION AT NIGHT at Palace Theatre, Watford.

28th July: British première of THE METEOR at Aldwych Theatre, London (see page 190).

Autumn: Dürrenmatt directs the Bochum version of FRANK V for North German Television (with Therese Giehse, Hubert von Meyerink, Hans Korte), broadcast on 16th February 1967.

Publication of collected SPEECHES AND WRITINGS ON THE THEATRE (*Theater-Schriften und Reden*).

1967 16th March: World première of THE ANABAPTISTS (*Die Wiedertäufer*) at Zurich Schauspielhaus (director: Werner Düggelin; designers: Teo Otto and Rudolf Heinrich; with Ernst Schröder, Gustav Knuth, Mathias Wieman, Walter Richter and Willy Birgel).

October: Dürrenmatt accepts regular post as full-time Director of the reorganised Basle Theatres from Season 1968–1969, working with Werner Düggelin. Plans for Basle include: a version of Aristophanes' *Archarnians* and a production of Goethe's *Urfaust*.

1968 February: Dürrenmatt gives lecture: '*Monster lecture on justice and law along with a Helvetian intermezzo. A miniature dramaturgy of politics*' (*Monstervortrag über Gerechtigkeit und Recht nebst einem helvetischen Zwischenspiel (Eine kleine Dramaturgie der Politik)*), in Mainz.

18th September: The 'Dürrenmatt-Düggelin' era begins at the Basle Theatres with the world première of KING JOHN (*König Johann. Nach Shakespeare*). Directed by Düggelin, with Horst Christian Beckmann as John.

November: British stage première of ONE AUTUMN EVENING (*Abendstunde im Spätherbst*) at Open Space Theatre, London (director: Frederick Proud; with Kenneth J. Warren).

1969 8th February: World première of PLAY STRINDBERG, adapted from Strindberg's *Dance of Death*. Directed by Dürrenmatt and Erich Holliger with Regina Lutz, Horst Christian Beckmann, Klaus Höring.

March: Dürrenmatt, with the publicist, Rolf R. Bigler, the historian Professor J. R. von Salis, and the writer Markus Kutter, becomes owner of the national-conservative 'Zürcher Woche' which, under Bigler's editorship and the new name 'Zürcher Sonntags-Journal', becomes a liberal weekly. Dürrenmatt, the author, contributes polemical articles, travel pieces and critical cultural essays, primarily related to Swiss domestic circumstances. (Dürrenmatt leaves the Sonntags-Journal in 1971. The paper ceases publication in autumn 1972.)

April: Dürrenmatt seriously ill.

8th May: CONVERSATION AT NIGHT televised by BBC-2 (director: Rudolph Cartier; with John Gielgud and Alec Guinness).

For his second Basle season, Dürrenmatt prepares a version of Lessing's MINNA VON BARNHELM, a free re-working of Shakespeare's TITUS ANDRONICUS and a new version of THE MARRIAGE OF MR MISSISSIPPI, which he will produce himself.

October: Outbreak of conflicts with the Basle directorate, smouldering for some time and fanned without a doubt by Dürrenmatt's own egocentricity. Main cause: Düggelin's rejection of the MINNA version and refusal to accept Dürrenmatt's demands for the casting of THE MARRIAGE OF MR MISSISSIPPI.

10th October: Dürrenmatt resigns and takes vehement

stock of the 'Basle experiment' in the Sonntags-Journal: 'I have to admit that, in this theatre of fools, I was the biggest fool.'

25th October: Dürrenmatt receives the Grand Prize for Literature of the city of Bern and provokes a scandal at the ceremony by handing over his prize to three left-wing radicals, Sergius Golowin, Paul Ignaz Vogel and Arthur Villard.

14th November: Receives the degree of Doctor of Literature from Temple University, Pennsylvania (see SENTENCES FROM AMERICA/*Sätze aus Amerika*, published 1970).

1970   Working on PORTRAIT OF A PLANET (*Porträt eines Planeten*). Dürrenmatt returns to the Zurich Schauspielhaus as free-lance artistic adviser to the new manager, Harry Buckwitz. First task: His own version and production of Goethe's URFAUST.

20th October: Première of URFAUST with Attila Hörbiger, Anne-Marie Kuster and Hans Helmut Dickow.

27th November: World première of PORTRAIT OF A PLANET (*Porträt eines Planeten*) at Kleines Haus, Düsseldorf (director: Erwin Axer; designer: Eva Starowieyska).

12th December: World première of TITUS ANDRONICUS, adapted from Shakespeare, at Düsseldorf Schauspielhaus (director: Karl-Heinz Stroux; designer: Heinz Mack; title rôle: Otto Rouvel).

1971   28th March: Première of Dürrenmatt's production of *Portrait of a Planet* (The so-called 'Zürich Version') at the Schauspielhaus.

1972   14th January: British première of PLAY STRINDBERG at the University Theatre, Newcastle-upon-Tyne.

17th February: Première of Dürrenmatt's production of Georg Büchner's *Woyzeck* at Schauspielhaus. Working on THE CONFORMER (*Der Mitmacher*).

1973   24th January: British première of PORTRAIT OF A
       PLANET at the Gardner Centre, University of Sussex
       by the Prospect Theatre Company. Subsequently
       toured to Cambridge, Southampton, Stirling, Glasgow
       Lancaster, Stockton-on-Tees and Leicester.
       8th March: World première of THE CONFORMER at
       Schauspielhaus. Dürrenmatt had quarrelled with the
       director, Andrzej Wajda shortly before the première
       and finally directs the performance himself.
       Widespread critical rejection of the play leads Dürren-
       matt to renounce playwriting for the time being.

1974   November: Visits Israel to receive honorary profes-
       sorship from the Ben-Gurion University.

1975   Protests against UNO's anti-Israel resolution at the
       P.E.N. conference in Vienna.

1976   October: British première of FRANK V by Theatr yr
       Ymylon, a Welsh touring company.
       1st–10th November: Visits Wales to receive Inter-
       national Writers' Prize 1976, from the Welsh Arts
       Council.
       CONNECTIONS (*Zusammenhänge: Eine Konzeption*) (on
       Israel journey) published, and text of *Der Mitmacher*,
       with appendices on drama.

1977   6th March: Receives Buber-Rozenweig Medal in
       Frankfurt from Society for Jewish-Christian Co-
       operation. Gives address on 'Tolerance'.
       6th October: World première of THE DEADLINE (*Die
       Frist*) at Zurich Schauspielhaus (director: Kasimierz
       Dejmek; designer: Andrej Mazewski).

I

Dürrenmatt's Work and Times

The *feeling* about the world which comes across in Dürrenmatt's works is an original, inexplicable intuition which takes precedence over any rational experience: man's feeling of smallness and impotence when faced with a chaotic, uncontrollable world which is 'a monstrosity, a problem which we must learn to live with but to which we must on no account capitulate'. In his theoretical pronouncements Dürrenmatt repeatedly connects this feeling with the state of the present-day world, with the terror implicit in mechanisms and organisations, with the intrusion of bureaucracy and technology into all forms of society, completely subjugating the powerless individual. Basically, however, these are only appearances in which an original sense of impotence finds itself confirmed, a helplessness which cannot be relieved by changing society but only by believing in a universally just and divine world order.

Just as fundamental as his 'pessimism' is Dürrenmatt's inclination for comedy. All his brilliant reasoning, which insists that comedy is the only type of drama suitable for the world in its present condition, is a subsequent rationalisation of a basic inclination. The peculiar feature of Dürrenmatt's style of drama resides in the vital pleasure he displays in things comical and grotesque set against the dark background of the world. On this rests his claim to independence, despite an affinity with the modes of expression used by Wedekind,

Wilder and Brecht. He follows authoritative models; the tragedy of Shakespeare, the comedy of Aristophanes. Tragedy is optimistic, comedy pessimistic (this is true of the classical theatre). Dürrenmatt goes beyond the limits of this typology because the conflicts which he presents in his comedies are essentially tragic, because the solutions which he offers his heroes, the downfalls which he prepares for them, are of tragic dimensions. Yet they are not tragic heroes: they stand and act only for themselves, not for the world, which (itself a comedy-world) is chaotic and remains irreconcilable. Tragic greatness is attained only by a few individuals who courageously stand firm against the chaos. 'The lost world-order is restored within them; the universal escapes my grasp' (*Problems of the Theatre*, p. 34).

Dürrenmatt is an Aristotelian – a fact which most clearly reveals his distance from Brecht – the contrast between tragedy and comedy, which hardly ever interested Brecht, stands at the centre of his dramatic philosophy. This deduces that comedy is necessary because tragedy is impossible; its starting point is therefore a declared deficiency – not in the theatre but in the world. Dürrenmatt's work (and equally his dramatic theory, which, although not systematically established, nevertheless, tends towards a system) strives constantly to bring a specific view of the world into congruence with a particular dramatic philosophy. Since his great dispute with Schiller (1959) Dürrenmatt's theoretical pronouncements on the quasi-historical, quasi-moral conception of a 'lost world-order' have increasingly been displaced by the completely ahistorical, amoral concept of 'Nature'. A play, he demands, shall be like a piece of nature – thus the world and the theatre are united; the standard postulate of bourgeois aesthetics, that art should interpret the world, is thereby settled. In order to make his position more precise Dürrenmatt develops an antithesis between 'Problem' and 'Conflict'; conflicts, mainly insoluble, are inherent in Nature (or in the world); on the other hand problems in nature only exist in the eye of the beholder. The discussion and solution of them should be left to the scientists and philosophers – art should be concerned with the presentation of conflicts, and these are timeless, even though, as for instance in *The Physicists*, they may be presented in thoroughly modern dress.

Although Dürrenmatt's works repeatedly seize upon the appearances of our civilised society, although he himself not only relates the form and style of these works to our age but even derives his theories from it, they are fundamentally neither an argument with nor an answer to this age. They present archetypal situations in modern dress and resolve archetypal conflicts under modern conditions. They are not concerned with the welfare state, the capitalist system or atomic war, but with responsibility, treachery, guilt, atonement, loyalty, freedom and justice: not with psychology, sociology, politics, but first and last, in the most absolute sense of the word, with morality.

Dürrenmatt does not preach a moral and does not assume a moralising attitude towards his characters. He is not their judge and does not use their fate to pass judgment on the world. 'I do not start with a thesis but with a story.' Dürrenmatt develops an idea, a basically theatrical situation, a conflict which contains its own rules within itself, into a story, into a theatrical world which is hermetic and self-absorbed. Lessons and evidence can only be drawn from it by people who project problems and solutions into it. 'Nor is it demanded of Nature that it should contain or even solve problems . . . the value of a play lies in the problems it poses, not in its simplicity.' A drama (that is, for Dürrenmatt, the theatre's potential and its duty) should disturb the spectator and provoke questions in him. Not questions about the play, but about himself, his own morality. Dürrenmatt's stories bring people in an immoral (nontragic) world into situations of conflict which force them into moral (tragic) decisions.

According to the essence of his dramatic philosophy, which
seeks not the relative but always and in every respect the
absolute, these conflicts are as basic as possible, of proportions as immense as possible, as it were 'larger than life'.
'Drama is first and last an attainment of the elementary.'
For Dürrenmatt this means that the theatre is a matter of
meaningful exaggeration, achieving its effects not with
nuances but with the strongest possible contrasts. Turning
points must not be subtly prepared but must happen in the
most direct and striking manner possible, the outlines must
not be blurred by psychological subtieties; rather the characters must be drastically typified by their physical appearances and manner of speaking. The distance between the
antagonists should be as extreme as possible; first and last,
king and beggar, judge and hangman, murderer and victim.

The theatricality of this world of superlatives is enormous,
so enormous that it sometimes appears impossible to expand
the collision between loyalty and treachery, between guilt
and atonement which is presented in it to the same scale.
Dürrenmatt's ideas, his premises, are incontestably cogent,
but their dramatic development can drive the antagonists into
such extreme positions that all moral categories are exploded.
They approach points beyond the dialectic of justice and
mercy where only rhetorical retreats are possible, because
dramatic necessity prescribes actions that are no longer
morally compelling. This explains why Dürrenmatt's plots
often have different endings in various versions. Only when
he had coped with the need to start with the 'idea' and write
'off into the blue', did Dürrenmatt get to grips with the
problem of bringing his arbitrarily developed plot to a con-
vincing conclusion. He postulates: 'A plot has been thought
out to the end only when it has taken its worst possible turning.' The play is then catapulted out of the realm of tragedy
into that of desperate farce.

A critical discussion of Dürrenmatt's plays cannot be an

exploratory assessment of the 'problems' they contain. Nor can it be a rhetorical interpretation and transfer of their morality to our world. It must take his own dramatic philosophy as the starting point, must investigate the necessity for and the consequences of the individual chess moves, must 'play the game over again' (Dürrenmatt) – this is the only way to estimate success or failure of a work, starting with Dürrenmatt's claim that: 'Providing something has a basis of truth then that truth will not fail to manifest itself.'

2

It is Written

The writer of this doubtful and from an historical view point downright insolent parody of the baptist kingdom [is none other than] a Protestant who is uprooted in the widest sense of the word, afflicted with the canker of doubt, mistrustful of the faith which he admires because he has lost it, a kind of mixture of sad phrases with a scurrilous delight in the improper.

In this contemptuous way Friedrich Dürrenmatt allows himself to be characterised and slandered by one of his stage-creatures, in a resolute attempt to acknowledge his own work and at the same time remain detached from it. *It is Written* is a drama in whose exaltations the author so emphatically reveals himself, that from time to time he has to bring down his protagonists in order to save himself from being overpowered by them. This does not happen without calculation; Dürrenmatt's way of tripping his characters up just when they are really

getting into their stride has method even in this first inordin-
ately grandiose play. Later he manipulates them more econo-
mically in order to produce greater areas of tension. In this
first play, the climaxes are violent and shortlived: to a certain
extent the play progresses from breaking point to breaking
point.

It is Written tells the story of the Anabaptist kingdom in
Münster in Westphalia (1533–6). The story of the journeyman
tailor Johann Bockelson from Leyden, who rose to become
king of the Anabaptists and after a short, terrible ascendancy
finished up as a heretic on the rack. Dürrenmatt is said to
have come across this, perhaps the most spectacular chapter
in the history of western millenarianism, during preliminary
researches for a dissertation. The play that he fashioned out
of it is neither parody nor history but is intended unmistakably as *theatrum mundi* in the baroque sense – a world theatre
whose language has its roots in the Old Testament psalms,
the Apocalypse, the German Mystics, and whose exagger-
ations and violent imagery betray the influence of Heym and
Trakl. Its expansive panoramic style seems to invite comparison with Claudel, but its grotesque comedy and uninhib-
ited delight in destroying all sublimity by an abrupt transition
to the ridiculous create from the first sentence onwards that
theatrical style with its exciting and irritating use of paradox
which is so typical of Dürrenmatt's work as a whole.

And, examined closely, the dramaturgic resources he has
here at his disposal for the realisation of his over-grandly
conceived design are still extremely limited. Time after time
he uses monologues, tirades and asides to let his characters
explain themselves to the audience. Time after time two of the
characters are put in extreme positions and set in battle
against each other, absolutely directly, point-blank, until at the
climax of the scene they change places or come together to
perform an 'antiphony'. Time after time the play switches
abruptly from the great to the small, from the sublime to the

grotesque. Happily for the play, these drastic dramatic techniques are just right for the excesses of the world it depicts.

When the curtain rises three psalm-chanting anabaptists are on their knees proclaiming in apocalyptic images the coming of their kingdom. The wretched appearance of these 'sober brethren' contrasts painfully with the magnificence of their language; yet it does possess a certain grandeur and recalls the song of the archangels in Goethe's *Faust*. Shortly afterwards someone else comes on. He has studied philosophy jurisprudence, medicine and theology; he is a road-sweeper, 'an impressive tramp', one of two 'Shakespearean' clowns who find the tattered prophet Johann Bockelson in a dung cart – supposedly the Archangel Gabriel has borne him from Leyden to Münster. (In the meantime, to bridge an embarrassing silence, the monk Maximilian Bleibeganz – 'I am not historical, I have never lived and have never regretted it' – has poked fun at the three anabaptists and has described the location of the action to the audience). Bockelson, half adopting his role and half standing outside it, introduces himself, announcing with a gracious gesture: 'We intend, by the way, to elevate ourselves to the position of Lord of the earth.' He enquires who is the richest man in the city, and the reply is: 'Have you never heard of Bernhard Knipperdollinck?' With that, the play about the poor Lazarus and rich man can begin.

Bockelson paints a mental picture of his meeting with Knipperdollinck ('He will just have eaten beans and bacon and for this reason he will be reading the Bible'), then as it were assumes the role of compère to announce the next scene to us. (Dürrenmatt frequently makes a character step out of his part so as to build a bridge from one scene to another.) Then Knipperdollinck in his turn introduces himself in an address to the audience: a godfearing man, for whom the biblical 'Woe unto you that are rich!' has deep meaning.

Bockelson enters with bold impudence – 'Am I not your
brother? Am I not poor Lazarus?' – and he gets what he
wants: food, clothing, soon even more. This is the first time
the antagonists have come together – by the end of Act One
they will have exchanged roles. After a conversation with the
Bishop, who should have been his opponent, but who in a
moment of weakness reveals himself as his brother ('Am I
greater than you that I should be able to grant you my blessing?'), Knipperdollinck does what the Bishop, strangely
exaggerating Christ's words to the point of paradox, has
advised him to do: 'Love thy enemies as thyself, sell all thou
hast and distribute unto the poor and do not resist evil.'

Dürrenmatt, however, is not concerned solely with telling
how Bockelson and Knipperdollinck exchanged fates, but
also with playing off a whole constellation of characters in
ever-shifting patterns against each other and thereby bringing
the topsy-turvy story of the anabaptist kingdom in Münster
onto the stage. Although time and again new major figures
introduce themselves in a speech to the audience and give
them up-to-date information on how things stand, the play
also includes a series of incidental scenes which do not so
much carry the action forward, as give information about its
progress: the seizing of power by the Baptists, the expulsion
of the Catholics and their Bishop, the mustering of an army in
the neighbourhood, the siege, the Baptists' first victory, and
so on. In order to convey this information to the audience,
Dürrenmatt uses methods which are well known from
Shakespeare's history plays: messenger's report; teichoskopia;
conversation between generals; dialogue between passers-by.
Yet he mistrusts such scenes, which by their very nature can
hardly be *dramatic* and attempts with a variety of methods to
theatricalise them. Two generals of the Catholic army, for
example, tell each other (and therefore the audience) in
alternating speeches about the siege plans. Dürrenmatt has
them act in the following manner: *'Their vizors are closed and*

must be raised every time a sentence is spoken, whereupon they fall down again and cover the speaker's face, which is only visible whilst he is actually speaking.' And, in order to bring into these exchanges of information a small degree of inner tension, Dürrenmatt makes them deadly enemies who have arranged a truce to last only for the duration of this campaign. The game with the vizors is comic, of course: one of the effects of stereotyped repetition, reversal and duplication which Dürrenmatt works into all his plays up to *The Physicists* with such sureness of instinct and such obvious delight. (In a later scene from *It is Written* the Hessian Duke Philip enters flanked by his two wives, who constantly utter the same sentence simultaneously with slightly altered word order.)

These scenes, serving only to illustrate the course of events, are used by Dürrenmatt above all to create contrasts, to destroy with clowning the effect of some grandeur recently shown and to create a comical situation from which some new grandeur can stand out effectively. Thus in the first Act the conversation between Knipperdollinck and the Bishop, one of the most unforcedly serious dialogues in the whole play, is followed 'immediately' (Dürrenmatt demands emphatically: 'immediately') by the vulgar spiel of a vegetable woman praising her lettuces ('as tender as sucking pigs' bottoms') and a grotesque execution scene. 'He's got an excellent right hand, our new executioner,' an expert citizen asserts. 'Let us hope that he will always have plenty of work to do. Only constant practice with real men will produce a perfect executioner.' And his daughter says ecstatically: 'Great! Look at those arms and legs. And such a fresh complexion. And what a forest he's got on his chest!' Or later: 'An executioner like that is like a god!' In this blasphemous way Dürrenmatt suddenly travesties one of the basic themes of the play. 'He is the sword and we are the body which is slain,' as the Bishop said shortly before about Christ.

The Second Act begins with four consecutive solo scenes.

Bockelson, prophet of a quite imminent 'Kingdom of God', who has taken possession of Knipperdollinck's house, his wife Katherine, and nine-tenths of his fortune, sings a voluptuous hymn praising the delights of his debauched existence. He is followed by Katherine, who bravely accepts her fate in a monologue: 'I know there will be much unhappiness and many tears, that for every pleasure despair awaits us, that the body which we love will be disfigured by the executioner's rack, and that the dogs playing at our gates will lick our blood.'

Then comes Judith, her daughter, who is leaving home to follow her father into poverty and distress: 'But I belong to him, even if I do not understand him.' Then, finally, Bockelson's new opponent the Baptist King, whom he intends to deprive of power:

> I, Jan Matthisson, emerge from the floor of this stage, raised by an ingenious device, the sword of justice in my hands and words of wisdom on my lips, to defend the holy cause, which here – and my face contorts with fury as I behold it – is being meanly debased and held up to public derision.

In the council of the Anabaptists the antagonists clash (their polarity is metaphorically associated with the sun and moon throughout the play). Matthisson wants to leave the defence of the city entirely to God; Bockelson ('If brother Matthisson thinks that the Old Man is going to bother himself personally . . .') calls for an armed struggle. The dramatic potential of such a scene seems to be of no interest to Dürrenmatt: he paints a colourless picture, a mere abbreviation of what happens. He gives much more rein to Bockelson who foretells the demise of his adversary, and trumpets forth on the city wall:

> But you lounging before me in this hall, witness now the death of the old prophet Matthisson, see now how the sun sinks into the sea of eternity. Cast your eyes up to the wall, where the

guard, his hands cupped to his mouth, turns towards you and
now begins to cry out in a mighty voice.

Time and again Dürrenmatt unconcernedly destroys the
potential effect of a visual incident by the monumentality of
the words he uses; for it would be impossible for a bit player
on a pasteboard cut-out to shout as powerfully as this speech
requires:

> Hot will be the battle, for the foe is mighty! Yet it is beautiful
> to drink the warm blood of the adversary! And the victorious
> city will be mirrored gloriously in the white corpses of its
> enemies who lie still on the earth, a pale carpet of death.

Such monumental rhetoric must be deflated by equally monumental triviality. A grotesque intermezzo drags the play down
to the level of a silly knock-about farce and, in so doing,
creates space for a new heroic crescendo: the magnificent
exit of Matthisson, who alone, 'bearing his sword before him
like a cross', strides out to meet the foe and death.

Then, bursting all limitations set by the stage, Dürrenmatt
heaps effect on effect. The enemy general urges on his men
with a rousing speech and announces that he will 'rise up
to be a giant and seize Mars, swinging my armoured right
arm towards heaven, so as to reduce the defiant city to dust
which will be blown away by the wind!' Bockelson, jumping
up from the orchestra pit 'raised aloft, projecting into the
audience and surrounded by it' seeks to surpass his opponent
with even more cosmic visions: 'See how the Heavens part
and He Himself, His countenance inflamed with rage, looks
on your enemies, about to hurl down bolts of lighting,
violently casting aside suns and worlds at His feet!' Yet
Dürrenmatt refrains from presenting this grandiosely in-
augurated battle. A musical interlude has to take the place of
what is no longer theatrically conceivable – 'which will do the
job far better than if the author undertook to set a few actors
loose upon each other with sticks and cardboard swords'.

One single character goes through the crude pantopticon of this play without ever being distorted into a monster or abandoned to ridicule (he does not actually 'go' but rather he is pushed in a wheelchair): the Bishop of Münster, 'ninety-nine years, nine months and nine days old', when he makes his first appearance in order to give the audience a short sermon, not in an apocalyptic tremolo, like all the prophets, but wisely, kindly and with infinite resignation:

> Believe me, the world can bear any wound and it generally does not matter whether or not man is happy, for happiness was not given to him, and if he has it he should regard it as an act of grace. It is necessary above all that he should stumble around on earth.

The Bishop has doubts about the church, which can achieve victory 'not with the Word but only with the stake'. He does not believe in its justice which is merely a 'pitiful intention to be just', and yet he performs the task which his role demands of him: he raises troops for the battle against the Baptists. Charles V appears, stiff as a statue (modelled exactly on the famous portrait by Titian), a ruler of the world who yearns for the anonymous solitude of a monk's cell – 'God created man in His own image and there are many in whom His goodness is manifested, and many who bear witness to His justice or His anger. In me, however, God buried the memorial to His remoteness and seclusion!' His master of ceremonies dusts the emperor down 'like an expensive piece of furniture', then the Bishop is pushed on stage and asks for military assistance. Dürrenmatt garnishes these exchanges with all sorts of grotesquely comic intermezzi, but that hardly covers up the fact that here are two versions of the same basic character; the Emperor's insight into his own impotence ('It is not we who control history: it is history which drags us through the ages') could also be that of the Bishop. In order to produce some tension between these two basically similar characters, Dürrenmatt transforms the Bishop, for this scene only, into an oily cleric. As the play proceeds, inconsistencies in the rôles, such 'changes in their polarity', are needed more and more, so as to create the antitheses.

One possible way of illustrating Bockelson's regime of pomp and terror consists in bringing him into collision with a variety of opponents drawn from an ideally inexhaustible store. For instance, with the traitor to whom, before he sentences him, he reveals his hedonistic faith 'in the empty sky, in this wall, in arms and legs, faces and hands and in the earth, bedded down under everything like a woman's body', and his awareness of fate: 'that is what it costs me – I am without hope. That is what weighs on me, that I might fall into a bottomless chasm.' This is followed by similar scenes where Bockelson orders mutinous women to be slaughtered, and where he changes roles with a sentry and, unrecognised by Katherine, kills her as she is trying to flee from the starving city. Repetition and accumulation, even of atrocities, have to replace the impossible peripeteia of this rambling and prolix drama.

For far too long, however, in fact throughout the middle Act, Knipperdollinck disappears. Now he appears again, 'his polarity having changed', in a new rôle which makes possible new groupings of characters. Bockelson has named him to be the governor of Zion: the judge of all the Baptists. It almost seems as if Dürrenmatt has given him this position only so that at the same time he can accomplish a new reversal of the extremes, theatrically to illustrate once more the proverb 'the first shall be last'. Knipperdollinck enters, the sword of justice in his hands, meets 'the most pitiable of the Baptists', a drunken nightwatchman, Vicomte Von Gê-Hinnon, hands him without hesitation the sword of justice – 'Who can be just? The first or the last, God or you, Vicomte?' – and strides off, now himself last again, a poor Lazarus. This scene could be the final culmination of a drama which has, strangely, shown varying characters amidst enduring principles. But the scene is too much of an abrupt cartoon to be more than an almost mechanical repetition of several grandiose, dramatised antitheses: Dürrenmatt is drawing breath for a last splendid tableau depicting the magnificence of King Bockelson.

Bockelson himself begins it with an enchantingly impudent hymn in praise of the delights of this earth:

> Praised be Blue Nun and Liebfraumilch! Praised be also pig's brawn and caviar, oysters and champagne, spit-roasted spring lambs stuffed with tiny Strasburg sausages, baked larks and the sweetbread of premature calves, together with the rich wine of Burgundy . . . chocolate cream, black pudding from Lower Saxony, potato salad and white beans with bacon, sour cider and a pie full of champignons, truffles, morels and emperor mushrooms, rice, Madeira sauce with capers, a Zizerser in precious crystal! Blessed and worshipped be what I have just enjoyed!

Bockelson is crowned, has his harem marched on stage, then his courtiers. He rules, divides the whole world among his princes and has Knipperdollinck, who how appears before him as 'poor Lazarus' (the two have not met since the first corresponding scene), thrown into the dungeon. The agony of the Baptist Kingdom begins, but Dürrenmatt does not tire of bringing his characters up against each other in still further combinations. Judith, Knipperdollinck's daughter, becomes Bockelson's mistress as a method of buying her father's freedom, but he wants to stay in the dungeon 'with my rats and my God'. Judith makes up her mind in a monologue which, according to the stage direction, 'echoes as if in the infinity of the universe': 'Judith came to Holofernes in the night and hacked off his head: Therefore I will go to the Bishop, who is surrounding Münster with terror, and kill him.' But the Bishop has seen into her heart, and she goes to her death with his blessing.

Once more the first and the last come face to face, Bockelson and Knipperdollinck. The one intoxicated with the world, the other intoxicated with God, now both fools in Christ, united in a grotesque antiphonal hymn to the moon: 'I hear the stone goats bleat in your valleys, I hear the cows lowing in your Alps, I hop with my paunch and wriggle my arse and dangle my arms.' They dance drunkenly through the palace, out of the window, over the edge of the roof, through the alleys – 'Let me dance into a world full of coconut palms and polar bears, of murderers singing at the gallows and of flowers sleeping on the hills!' – on out of the city gate. Münster is taken and devastated. In triumph the victorious Duke of Hesse surveys his works:

> Doesn't it bring it all home to you, eternal agony, doesn't everything come crashing down on you, bottomless abyss!
> THE BISHOP. The point of it all lies in their agony, Duke of Hesse.
> DUKE (*as he goes out slowly*). Woe to them that have lost God.
> THE BISHOP. Hail to him who finds Him on the rack again.

After a final clown-interlude with the road-sweeper who carts off Bockelson's corpse these two are standing before Knipperdollinck: bound to the rack and dying, he submits to the will of God: 'Everything which happens reveals Thine eternity, Lord! The depth of my despair is merely an image of Thy justice, and my body lies on this rack as if in a dish which Thou fillest to the brim with Thy Grace.'

The grandeur and extravagance of this play are astonishing: a stroke of genius, a challenge to the theatre, thoroughly individualistic, a first outline of Dürrenmatt's world, in which much has already been mapped out which can never again be dissociated from it; road-sweepers, cooks and executioners who play with quotations from the classics; giants who founder on the absoluteness of their aspirations; faithful fools who recognise God's greatness in their downfall; and, in the

B

figure of the Bishop, the hero of self-conquest, of renunciation, and of moderation in a confused world.

3

The Blind Duke

Dürrenmatt's tendency, not to say method, of jumping from one extreme to another can be seen in the zigzag progress of his work; a concentric play is always followed by an eccentric one; so the unrestrainedly rambling spectacle *It is Written* which bursts asunder all the shackles binding the theatre, is followed by the concise drama, *The Blind Duke*, which is characterised by its strictly controlled theatrical effects. A single place of action, a single plot progressing in a straight line, no provocative punches below the belt, no ironic somersaults, no shattering of the theatrical reality and no stepping out of character. (When Dürrenmatt said of *The Physicists* that it was the first of his plays to conform to the demands of the Aristotelian unities, he seems to have forgotten *The Blind Duke*.) The clear, sharply defined structure of this second play is certainly a surprise after the (apparently) riotous and reckless accumulation of scenes in his first play, but Dürrenmatt does not achieve the stringency demonstrated here without noticeable strain. *The Blind Duke* is a grandly conceived play which in practice falls considerably short of the aspirations of its design.

The Christian text of which we must take *The Blind Duke* to be the exposition has already been quoted in *It is Written*: 'Lord, Lord, hast Thou not helped those who believed in

Thee? Hast Thou not spoken thus to the blind: "It will happen to you according to your faith"?' And a minor character in that play was a blind man who recognises that he must believe everything that people tell him if he does not want to doubt and despair of everything. It is that and that alone, which constitutes the subject-matter of *The Blind Duke*: the unshakeable faith of a blind man, not only in all the things which people tell him about but also in the divine justice which manifests itself in those things.

An old Duke, Lear and Job rolled into one, blinded as a result of an illness, sits in front of the ruins of his castle in a country ravaged and devastated by the Thirty Years' War. But because, out of compassion, his son has refrained from telling him of all the destruction, the Duke believes that, with God's grace, he is ruling happily and peacefully over a happy people. The 'Tempter' appears, one of Wallenstein's generals by the name of Negro da Ponte, and recognises the significance of the Duke's 'faith' from his words. When the blind Duke appoints him as his governor, Da Ponte determines to destroy the Duke's 'faith' by resorting to mean trickery, to plunge him into despair by revealing the 'truth'. (Even this first dialogue is full of direct allusions to the meeting between Job and the Devil.)

With the aid of his hangers-on, Negro da Ponte dramatises, as a sort of radio-play, what has been concealed from the blind Duke: the collapse of his realm. A strolling player offers his services to the Duke as a French chevalier, a whore makes her entrance as the abbess of a destroyed convent and asks for asylum; then Negro da Ponte announces that Wallenstein's army is approaching and advises the Duke to flee. All day long the 'chevalier' leads the Duke round and round the ruins; thus they enact 'flight into the mountains' and later 'return to the ruined castle', where a drunken negro in the rôle of Wallenstein awaits the Duke and accepts his solemn gesture of submission.

'A model theatrical situation: the point of the play lies wholly in the interplay of perception and imagination. Here the theatre is playing itself,' wrote Max Frisch about *The Blind Duke* after the première. And Dürrenmatt himself wrote in 1954: 'In *The Blind Duke* I was concerned to juxtapose the word with the dramatic location, to test the word against the visual image.' To test the word against the visual image (the phrase is exactly right) means: to place faith in God's justice as against senseless chaos and to let the one 'test' the other. He who sees must despair. In *It is Written*, the imaginative power of his language was a danger for Dürrenmatt: the words conjured up images which the stage was incapable of realising. In *The Blind Duke*, on the other hand, where the pointless contradiction between word and pictorial image is replaced with great success by antithesis, he could develop the language without restraint. But strangely enough it does not work. Where he intends his language to be lapidary, it is often merely impoverished; often where he aims at grandeur, he simply ends up debasing big words (cursing and blessing; life and death; truth and falsehood); where the 'credo quia absurdum' (I belive it because it is absurd), the paradox of faith, is supposed to be expressed, the paradox often acts as a mere auxiliary rhetorical device. The ambivalence of the play is made superficial by *double entendre*.

THE WHORE. I used to be the abbess of a convent.

THE DUKE. Where was this holy house?

THE WHORE. In Munich in Bavaria. We devoted ourselves to the service of love. We were never unwilling. We were always ready to place ourselves at the disposal of those who needed us. Nobody went from us without having found relief. Through our love we made many people happy.

THE DUKE. So you sacrificed yourself for love.

THE WHORE. I sacrificed day and night.

THE DUKE. Love is not in vain, duchess.

THE WHORE. We never love for nothing.

THE DUKE. Why did you leave your convent?
THE WHORE. We were overpowered.
THE DUKE. You are now on the run?
THE WHORE. I am driven from one general to another.
THE DUKE. Times are bad outside my country.
THE WHORE. Soldiers are always getting on top of one.

This is witty but very strained, very laboured.

Where Dürrenmatt tries to play with words like Shakespeare's or Büchner's fools and melancholics the result is often nothing but pert and graceless sophistry:

NEGRO DA PONTE. I am pleased to have come across you, my Prince.
PALAMEDES. You have crossed me already. You have made my sister into a whore.
NEGRO DA PONTE (*draws his sword*). It is only fair that I should fight you.
PALAMEDES. You are right. You are fighting with a fair weapon. You have wounded me with a woman.
NEGRO DA PONTE. You are witty.
PALAMEDES. I like jokes with sharp points.
NEGRO DA PONTE. I shall run the sharp point of your joke through your body.

To be fair, there *are* more successful exchanges in the play, repartee which makes the sparks fly:

SUPPE. You are bitter, my Prince.
PALAMEDES. You mean, the world is bitter – a common view. Do you like riddles?
SUPPE. Very much, my Prince.
PALAMEDES. Is God just or unjust?
SUPPE. Unjust, my Prince.
PALAMEDES. Just, my court poet; otherwise the world would not be hell.

Negro da Ponte, the Tempter, the 'God incarnate', does not only play with the blind Duke but also with his children Palamedes and Octavia. Palamedes, the melancholy prince

who uses lies to keep alive his father's 'faith' and therefore
calls himself 'God', does not interfere with da Ponte because
he himself is curious to see the outcome of the experiment;
but suddenly he too is compelled to take a rôle in the play.
Negro da Ponte accuses him in front of the Duke of having
betrayed his dukedom to Wallenstein. Palamedes, dismayed
at the unshakeable faith of his father, tries by a final lie,
which ultimately condemns him, to put this faith right. He
admits the betrayal, and the blind Duke sentences him to
death. Negro da Ponte hands him over to the hangman. This
'baroque' reversal from play-acting to deadly earnest, from
lie to truth (for Palamedes has indeed betrayed his father, not
to Wallenstein, but to Negro da Ponte) turns the play, which
despite all the stylisation had the psychological makings of
a father–son drama, into an allegory of the Passion; the
biblical references in the speeches by the 'Satan', Negro da
Ponte ('I embrace everything which falls into my hands'), and
by the 'God/father' ('By your death you are mine again')
are impossible to overlook. But Palamedes is not Christ.
Dürrenmatt's theology being almost paradoxical, he stages
the Passion of Judas. Palamedes has lost his faith, but he has
not escaped God; as he dies, he reveals to his sister Octavia,
who hates their father: 'Why do you want to be cursed when
our father blesses you, and why do you want to be guilty
when our father pardons you? . . . You can deny him, but
you still belong to him. The more you curse him the stronger
become the ties that bind you to him. For your father remains your father.'

From a dramatic point of view, Octavia is the weakest
character, a pathetic embodiment of a philosophy which at
the time, 1948, was very much in fashion: Sartre's existenti-
alism. Octavia hates her father, despises her brother and gives
herself to Negro, 'the man who scorns my father and strikes
my brother. For he strikes what I had to reject before I could
live, and he scorns what was my prison.' Negro da Ponte has

released her from this prison, and it is from him she borrows her words: 'I act as I am. I belong to no one but myself. I believe in nothing. I am free.' But this 'nihilistic' feeling of freedom is a brief intoxication which is followed by the endless hangover of despair. Proudly she opposes her dying brother: 'I bear the guilt, and I seek no pardon. I reject the blessing and reach for the curse. I use my hate like a shield against my father's love.' But a little later she complains: 'I am so without grace, without hope, without faith! How forlorn I am now, now no one has found me!' And she calls to her father: 'I have broken your law, I have cursed your name and I have betrayed you. I will now be cursed according to your law and from my hands falls a tattered banner – hate.' The blind Duke appears (by chance), yet Octavia does not throw herself at his feet but disappears without a word, following not an inner, ideal law, but simply external dramatic necessity.

What Dürrenmatt perhaps intended with this counterpart to the Orestes of *The Flies*, namely a refutation of Sartre's philosophy of freedom, is successful only in theatrical terms. Octavia's precipitation into naked despair is not something forced on her by the nature of the character she is playing, but it is necessary for the final climax, the turning-point of the play. The working out of the final scene, the ultimate revelation of the truth which is to cast the Duke into despair, poses foreseeable problems. For Negro da Ponte cannot in any real way 'open the Duke's eyes', cannot show him that the abbess was a whore, that Wallenstein was a Negro and therefore that their every word was a lie; he has only one means of destroying the blind Duke's faith which was based on words; and that is words. Words, which can only contradict but cannot entirely refute those already spoken.

Dürrenmatt resolves this dilemma with remarkable inspiration and yet makes possible a 'tangible' destruction of the 'faith in words'. The Poet Laureate Gnadenbrot Suppe (the only comic-grotesque marginal character who crops up in the play without much apparent function beyond providing contrasts) wants to reveal to the Duke the 'truth of one who can see', but the Duke does not listen to him and instead reveals to him the 'truth of one who is blind.' As he strangles Suppe, the Duke says: 'O sacred blindness, you water over which I stride, you sea over which I wander.' Now Negro da Ponte causes this corpse to be covered and brought before the blind Duke with the explanation that it is Octavia, who has committed suicide. 'Then welcome,' says the Duke, 'you have become my burden, the guilt which I bear, the punishment which I suffer, the justice which has been done to me and the hope of grace which never leaves me.' This is Negro da Ponte's big moment; 'I give you what you have never wanted and I show you what you have never seen: the truth. I compel you to judge between this truth and your faith, for I place you face to face with it like an adversary who has come to kill you.' He tells the blind Duke the truth about his castle, and his dukedom, about Wallenstein and the abbess, and finally about the corpse at his feet:

So grasp what lies before you, reach for the corpse which has been brought to you, dare to reach out for its face, blind man! Into the face of a dead man, into this waxen flesh that still stinks of liquor although it is dead, into this effigy of your absurdity, into this proof that Octavia is alive, into this answer to your faith, which I now unveil before you!

So far so good. But 'he draws the cloak from the body and Octavia is revealed' ('We did not need any Poet Laureate,' declares Negro's assistant; 'Octavia killed herself right in front of me'). And Negro da Ponte, whose truth has thus become falsehood, capitulates to the blind Duke: 'It has happened to you according to your faith.' At this moment Dürrenmatt's allegory, so grandly designed, collapses; the bold equation of religious faith and 'faith' in the sense of 'trust', of 'taking to be true', no longer holds good. No dramatic moment in Dürrenmatt's work relates more forcibly than this collapse to his statement: 'The difficulties experienced by a Protestant with the art of drama are exactly the same difficulties that he has with his faith,' and to the slightly resigned insight that 'a Catholic dramatist has possibilities not open to any other': the Miracle and the Redemption.

> What lay between Man and God is smashed in pieces. The greatness of man lies in fragments all around us and the way we must go is blasted in our flesh as if in a rock face. Thus we have received what is due to us. Thus we are sent back to the place which we must occupy. Thus we lie shattered in the sight of God and thus we live in His truth.

These final words of the Duke have seriousness, greatness, poetic power. *It has happened to him, according to his faith, but not, in my view, through God but through a coup de théâtre.*

4

Romulus the Great

The Bishop, Knipperdollinck and the blind Duke are ridiculous in the sight of God and man, and they are conscious of their absurdity. But they are laughed at only by the characters on stage – not by the audience. The incongruity of this effect might have been an additional reason for Dürrenmatt to call into question his attempt to create a drama rooted in the Protestant faith. When it is obvious that God is the final arbiter to whom the business on the stage is to be referred, a modern audience, indifferent to religion, will feel in duty bound to be deeply moved by an edifying spectacle and hyper-sensitive to an ostensibly blasphemous one. In either case, its reaction stems from feelings of emotional insecurity and is not spontaneous or naïve. Such a reaction is hardly even possible for an audience confronted with a play like *The Blind Duke*, where, to quote Frisch again, the theatre is in fact 'playing itself'. In this case it is playing a game *with* itself, and the audience has no chance to get involved. Dürrenmatt's early plays neither take into account nor involve the audience, the most essential element in the whole concept of theatre. Not until *Romulus the Great* does he discover the one, perhaps the only, possible way of getting the amorphous theatre audi-ence of today into the palm of his hand: through the unifying power of laughter.

We can laugh freely at Romulus, perhaps not least because here the authority which governs his actions is not God, but the unambiguous immediacy of 'world history'. When two rather comical emperors sit down 'in an attitude of devotion' and, as it were with bated breath, affirm their faith in their 'historic mission', nobody senses blasphemy. There is laughter when one of them assures the other: 'A marvellous feeling, is it not? One can positively feel the positive power charging these rooms!' Romulus resolutely rejects the idea of enlisting God's aid: 'I don't know whether God is on our side. In-formation on that is rather vague.' Romulus has a deep and unconditional *faith* in his 'historic mission'. In contrast to those who merely keep talking about it Romulus is resolved to sacrifice his life to its fulfilment. As the last Western Roman Emperor his conception of 'patriotic duty' is totally different from that of all who surround him: his wife, his daughter, his ministers of state and his soldiers.

The action of this 'unhistorical historical comedy' takes place on the Ides of March 476. A German army under

Odoaker is marching triumphantly through northern Italy towards Rome; but the Emperor does what he has been doing for the past twenty years: precisely nothing. He sits in his villa in Campania rearing chickens: calmly and cheerfully he derives great amusement from the panic-stricken antics of his 'responsible' underlings. Throughout the First Act more and more ominous tidings of disaster keep coming in. Romulus, however, sits comfortably eating his breakfast, with all the time in the world to spare, and reacts to all the catastrophes with unshakeable good humour. In a fit of righteous indignation his fellow-sovereign reproaches him: 'Amazing. A whole world goes up in flames and you make silly jokes.'

The play opens, before the Emperor has stirred from his bed and made his appearance, with the arrival of a messenger of doom. Spurius Titus Mamma, Captain of the Cavalry, has ridden 'his horse at the gallop two days and two nights' to announce the Germans' conquest of Pavia and the surrender of the last Roman army – but the two 'ancient, grey and immovable chamberlains, standing like statues', are imperturbable and tell the exhausted messenger that he must observe protocol and seek an audience: 'perhaps then, in the course of the next few days, you may be able to deliver your news personally to the Emperor'. Spurius staggers out in despair: 'Unhappy Rome! Two chamberlains are your downfall!' This pithy scene sets out the whole situation, creates the tension from which the first Act draws its inspiration. The Emperor appears, cheerful, good-natured, and enquires not about the state of his empire but about his (not very productive) hens, which bear the names of his predecessors. He then starts his breakfast.

But he is not allowed to eat in peace. First the Minister of the Interior enters and asks the Emperor to grant an audience to Captain Spurius. (Romulus replies: 'Lead him to the quietest guest-chamber in my house, Tullius Rotundus. Even athletes must sleep.') Next, showing pathetic concern, the Empress Julia makes the same request. Romulus refuses:

> As the father of my country I will probably be Rome's last Emperor. For that reason alone, I occupy a rather forlorn position in world history. No matter what happens I shall end up with a bad reputation. But there is one bit of fame no one shall take from me: no one shall ever say that I had wilfully disturbed the sleep of any man unnecessarily.

Finally the Minister of War is the third to demand an audience for the Captain, but by this time the Emperor has his mind on another announcement, which he finds more interesting: he has just been told that the hen called Odoaker has laid a third egg. And he concludes: 'The ruler of the Teutons, Odoaker, has conquered Pavia. I know this is so because the hen bearing his name has just laid three eggs . . . Without this natural harmony, there would be no order in the world.' A mood of catastrophe reigns but Romulus proposes: 'I will issue a communiqué that I am in good health.' Calmly he goes on negotiating with the art-dealer Apollonius to whom he wants to sell the busts of his predecessors, to put off for one more day the 'bankruptcy of the Roman Empire'.

Of course, there is a method in the Emperor's madness: he plays the buffoon deliberately, because he is convinced that this is the best thing to do. When he declares to his daughter Rea, who, as a drama student, is learning the role of Antigone: 'Why study that old tragic text? Why not comedy? It's more fitting for our time,' – then he is not only expressing Dürrenmatt's dramatic credo but also making his own confession of faith: 'People whose number is up, like us, can only understand comedy.'

Zeno the Isaurian, the Eastern Roman Emperor, comes in and asks for asylum. Romulus however keeps up the comedy:

ZENO. We cannot afford the luxury of petty suspicions between our two empires. We must save our culture.

ROMULUS. Why? Is culture something anyone can save?

The Emperor refuses to take the downfall of his empire seriously and cracks jokes about the man who now approaches as rescuer: the trouser manufacturer from Germany, Caesar Rupf.

'I am, of course, also one hundred per cent aware that Rome's conservative circles are against trousers, just as they are against everything else that dawns new on the horizon,' says Caesar Rupf; and Romulus counters: 'Where trousers commence, culture ends.' But Rupf, 'a man of unclouded realism', knows 'A modern state whose citizens do not wear trousers will go to pot', and proposes a deal to the Emperor: 'Let us call a diamond a diamond, not tarnished by any sentimentalities. Behind me stand a few million sesterces; behind you, the deluge.' For ten million, paid by Rupf, the Germans are ready to clear out of Italy: the Emperor's part of the bargain is that he shall make trousers obligatory and give Rupf the hand of his daughter, Rea, in marriage. 'It is as clear as day that only in this way can the alliance be cemented organically.' But Romulus declines:

ROMULUS. I will sell the Roman Empire for a handful of sesterces here and now, but I have not the faintest intention of bargaining away my daughter.

JULIA. Rea will voluntarily sacrifice herself for the empire.

ROMULUS. For centuries, we have sacrificed much to the state. Now it is time for the state to sacrifice itself for us.

JULIA. Romulus!

ZENO. If your daughter does not marry him now, the world will come to an end.

ROMULUS. We will come to an end. That's quite a difference.

ZENO. We are the world.

ROMULUS. We are provincials for whom the world has grown too large. We can no longer comprehend it.

These are programmatic sentences: Romulus knows what he wants. Removing his fool's cap, he says frankly to Captain Spurius, who finally re-appears to conclude the accelerating succession of entrances: 'Rome died long ago. You are sacrificing yourself for a corpse. You are fighting for a shadow. The country you live for is no more than a grave. Go to sleep, Captain, our times have turned your heroism into a pose.'

In this brilliantly constructed and executed exposition Dürrenmatt reveals himself for the first time as a dramatist who calculates every effect with certainty, who commands the stage. Right up to *The Visit* it is his first acts which are always the best; they set the plays in motion with so much verve that they must of necessity be followed by a ritardando. The second act of *Romulus* begins in a particularly jerky fashion because without Romulus the play lacks a centre, the stable core around which the action can revolve with increasing turbulence. Spurius is still not asleep, the Minister of War is arming for the final battle, the Minister of the Interior is organising the flight to Sicily, Rea is reciting Sophocles with her teacher – it all contributes peripherally to the fun. That is, until Emilian, Rea's fiancé, appears, having escaped from the Germans after three years as a prisoner of war, so disfigured by tortures that nobody, not even Rea, can recognise him. He (and he is the only one) has the moral right to call for a last act of resistance and to demand of Rea that she sacrifice herself when Caesar Rupf appears demanding a final answer to his 'fundamentally honest offer': 'Yes or no. Wedding feast or world defeat.' Rea replies to Emilian: 'If you really loved me, you would not ask this of me.' But Emilian says: 'I can ask this of you only because you love me.' Rea is ready, offers her hand to the 'coolly determined' trouser manufacturer. Jubilation breaks out – and wakens Romulus from his midday snooze. Emilian greets him scornfully: 'Welcome O Caesar of the good dinner-table. Greetings unto you, Emperor of fine fowl. Hail unto you whom your soldiers call Romulus the Little.' But Romulus, who is the only one to recognise Emilian at once, greets him earnestly and, as he realises the situation, declares with ceremonial solemnity: 'The emperor will not permit this marriage,' for 'The Emperor knows what he is doing when he throws his Empire into the flames, when he lets fall what must break, when he grinds under foot what is doomed.'

The final line of Act One was: 'Emperor, you're a disgrace to Rome.' Emilian concluded Act Two with 'Down with the Emperor!' Now, in the Third Act, in an almost classical bedroom farce, the fate of the imperial chicken-breeder is to be sealed in accordance with the tradition of the Ides of March. But first this 'Judge of the world disguised as a fool' is allowed to justify himself before world history, that is, before its representative authority: the public. The Empress Julia comes to him to say farewell. He is already in his dressing-gown and is enjoying finishing off his last bottle of Falernian wine. And now he reveals to his wife why he became Emperor, why he married her: to 'have the opportunity to liquidate the empire'.

JULIA. You acted the cynic and the perpetual over-stuffed buffoon in order to stab us in the back? . . . You are Rome's traitor.

ROMULUS. No, Rome's judge.

Rea appears and asks once more to be allowed to marry Caesar Rupf, but Romulus is 'not like that sire of heroes in one of your tragedies who says "good appetite" to the State when the State wants to devour one of his children. Go, marry Emilian!' he says to Rea. 'Can you live without your beloved? To remain loyal to a human being is greater and much more difficult than to remain loyal to a State.' Rea replies: 'It is my country, not just a State.' Romulus: 'Every State calls itself "country", or "nation", when it is about to commit murder.' Then he takes his leave: 'The Teutons will kill me. I have always counted on that death. That is my secret. I sacrifice Rome through sacrificing myself.'

Romulus did not have this secret when he appeared on the stage for the first time in 1949. The introduction and development of this new idea is the most significant addition in the revised version of 1957. It reveals – more significantly than the greater concision, the more powerful pointing of the dialogue – the extent to which Dürrenmatt's sureness of touch had developed. He no longer seeks to create contrast and effect through the groupings of characters in individual scenes, but through the characters themselves. Not until the sacrifice-motif has been introduced is the figure of Romulus rounded off; only then can it be said to be fully thought-out, and its extremity justified: 'A dangerous fellow, a man determined to die', not a traitor but a judge. When Rea has gone, Romulus calls out to Emilian, whom he has observed climbing in through the window. Then, suddenly, black-cloaked conspirators come creeping from every possible hiding-place: the Minister of the Interior, Zeno with his retinue, Spurius Titus Mamma, the Minister of War. Romulus watches this charmingly comic procession quite calmly, but then, 'for the first time, the Emperor is visibly moved', when the Cook, complete with white hat, comes out from beneath the divan: 'You, too, Cook?' Romulus knows how to treat the moment with the seriousness it deserves: he calls for his imperial toga and laurel wreath and then solemnly renders his account, not to Rome but to the only person to whom he is indebted: Emilian.

> For me you represent the final great argument against those who, like myself, refuse to defend themselves; in you I'm willing to see the militant challenge of the people violated again and again, the victims of power defiled a thousand times.

Romulus defends himself whilst accusing Rome, the tyranny of the world empire, 'the mound of human sacrifices' on which his 'invisible throne' stands, this pyramid of skulls down whose steps cascade rivers of blood in endless waterfalls, generating Rome's power . . . Answer my question now: Do we still have the right to defend ourselves? Do we still have the right to be more than victims?

Emilian and all around him answer by drawing their swords. Romulus would be doomed if, at this moment, there did not come 'from the back, a horrifying cry of fright: "The Teutons are coming!" ' They all scatter in panic. But Romulus climbs calmly into bed, over the body of Spurius: 'Heavens be thanked. Our athlete is asleep at last.'

Next morning Romulus is alone: everybody has left him, and all – Julia, Rea, Emilian, the Ministers, the Cook – have drowned on the crossing to Sicily. Romulus has settled accounts with life: 'Never was I more composed. Never more cheerful than now, when it is all over.' He dismisses his servants and sits down to his last meal: the last egg, the last asparagus wine. But Romulus has miscalculated. This determined fool, this convinced do-nothing, who considers it a crime to put a dislocated era back into joint, this well-fed anti-Hamlet is confronted by a Fortinbras who demands that he remain in highest office. His plans collapse in ruins about his head: Odoaker is there not to kill him but to place himself at his disposal. Like Romulus he is a determinedly unheroic man, a romanophile with a penchant for classical antiquity and, above all, a chicken-breeder. They could be friends if they were not facing one another as victor and vanquished, and if the victor were not so obstinate in his insistence on subjugating himself to the vanquished.

Romulus wants to be killed, Odoaker wants him to be Emperor over his Teutons, whose warmongering power-lust he fears. But now both have been cheated: Romulus of his sacrificial death, his only means of justifying the sacrifice of his Empire; Odoaker of his hope of out-manœuvring his terrible nephew, 'who some day shall be called Theodoric the

Great, if I know those historians'. They know that 'a second Rome will rise, a Teutonic empire, as transitory as Rome and as bloody', and they acknowledge their impotence: 'We thought we could drop the world from our hands – you, your Germania and I, my Rome. Now we must busy ourselves with the pieces that are left.' Romulus is ready to bear his guilt and go into retirement. Odoaker will reign benevolently until his nephew kills him. 'Let us bear this bitterness. Let's try to endow the nonsense with sense! Try in the few years which will still be yours to rule the world faithfully. Give peace to the Teutons and to the Romans alike,' Romulus urges his successor.

> Maybe they will be a few years which world history will forget because they will be unheroic years – but they will be amongst the happiest this confused world has ever lived through . . . Once more and for the last time, let us play this comedy. Let us act as if final accounts were settled here on earth, as if the spirit won over the material called man.

So they go before their troops, execute the discharge of power; then (because the play is supposed to be a comedy, after all) Spurius Titus Mamma, awake at last, rushes in with sword drawn, only to learn that there is no longer an Emperor: 'Then the last imperial officer slept right through the fall of his homeland!'

In no comedy of Dürrenmatt's does his stoic faith, his fatalistic view of history stand out more clearly than in this witty and profound end-of-the-world farce; he has equipped none of his heroes with so much sincerity, superior humour and undisguised humanity as:

> this judge of the world disguised as a fool. His tragedy lies in the comedy of his end; instead of a sacrificial death, he has earned for himself retirement. But then – and this alone is what makes him great – he has the wisdom and the insight to accept his fate.

The distance between the Emperor, who in his wisdom flees into a chicken house and plays the fool, and the Physicist, who in his wisdom flees into a lunatic asylum and plays the madman, is not all that great. Both are deceived and their sacrifice is robbed of its point – but what we cannot do is *laugh* at Möbius.

5

The Marriage of Mr Mississippi

That he was concerned to investigate what happens when certain ideas collide with people who really take them seriously and strive with audacity and vigour, with insane fervour and an insatiable desire for perfection, to put them into effect . . .

This was Dürrenmatt's intention in *The Marriage of Mr Mississippi*, or so we are assured by one of his heroes, Count Übelohe, 'the only one whom he [the author] loved in all his passion, because I alone in this play take upon myself the adventure of love, that sublime enterprise which, whether he survies or perishes in it, endows man with his greatest dignity'. And furthermore we learn 'that the curious author sought an answer to the question of whether the spirit – in any shape or form – is capable of changing a world that merely exists and is not informed by any idea, and that he wished to ascertain whether or not the material universe is suceptible of improvement'. The answer which Dürrenmatt – this 'lover of gruesome fables and futile comedies . . . this stubborn Protestant with his morbid imagination' – uses this play to provide, is quite unmistakable: the world is the undoing of every man; it is what it is, unchangeable and indestructible.

The comedy – the theatrical experiment which leads to this conclusion – returns to the high-flown expressive language of Dürrenmatt's first plays and exaggerates it to the extent of parody: its boundless rhetoric elevates what seems to be a drawing-room thriller to the level of allegory. Not only is the language of this comedy incongruously bombastic but also, ingeniously and consistently, the décor, the characters, the intrigues, the effects, even the proper names, down to the maid, who is called Lucretia. This is the 'story of a room', Dürrenmatt declares quite simply in the description of the scene. 'Really the main character in the play' is a Biedermeier coffee table. The late bourgeois splendour of the room, which is packed with furnishings from all over the world and of all periods, is meant to 'stink to high heaven'; the views from the windows are, to the right, 'some northern city with a Gothic cathedral' and, to the left, 'a cypress, the remains of a classic temple, a bay, a harbour'. A showplace of the world, then – at least, of the West.

The play begins with a bang, a *coup de théâtre*: three men dressed in raincoats with red armbands shoot a fourth man and disappear. The one who has just been shot, in evening dress, with red socks, turns to face the audience and explains that this is the end of the play, brought forward 'for therapeutic reasons' but now they will begin in the right order and relate

> the somewhat regrettable fate of three men, who for various reasons, had taken it into their heads to change and save the world and who then had the appalling bad luck to run into a woman who could neither be changed, nor saved, because she loved nothing but the moment.

Such speeches to the audience, elucidating the action and explaining its course (often like a *Moritat*, with the aid of large placards), are repeated as the play progresses; they replace ('like the chorus in Greek tragedy', according to Dürrenmatt) the curtain between the individual acts. The three men above-mentioned, who are frantically trying to change and redeem the world are:

Florestan Mississippi, the Public Prosecutor, obsessed with the idea of re-introducing the Law of Moses 'in all its terrible greatness'. Fanatical supporter of an inhumanly absolute, 'divine' justice, 'the most hated man in the world'.

Frédéric René Saint-Claude, professional revolutionary Communist. Fanatical supporter of an earthly justice.

Count Bodo von Übelohe-Zabernsee, pious parish doctor. Fanatical supporter of humility and charity, 'a last Christian'.

The woman whom these three personified philosophies meet and on whom they founder is Anastasia, 'not modelled upon heaven or hell, but only upon the world', an exaggerated version of Wedekind's Lulu, 'a woman who consumes an immoderate quantity of men' – Dame World (Frau Welt) and Whore of Babylon at the same time. The play begins (after the prologue with the shooting of Saint-Claude and his speech to the audience) with the first, solemn encounter between Anastasia and Mississippi. Both are in mourning: she has lost her husband a few days before (a heart attack), he his wife (a heart attack). Over a cup of coffee, Mississippi reveals to Anastasia in an extremely formal manner that both the deceased were adulterers – 'We have been deceived by your dead husband François and my dead wife Madeleine' – and wrests from Anastasia with cunning and threats the admission that she not only knew of this but also that she poisoned her husband when he was having a cup of coffee after his lunch (the poison, similar in appearance to a lump of sugar – Mississippi knows for a fact – she had obtained surreptitiously from her childhood friend, Übelohe). This conversation has a 'frightful' effect, not because of the revelations it brings but because they both continuously assert its frightfulness – the dialogue is positively bristling with adjectives like 'monstrous', 'terrible', 'awful', 'dreadful', 'insane'; 'torment' and 'hell' are evoked, and there are even stage directions like 'filled with horror', 'deathly pale', 'shuddering', 'stunned', 'white-faced', 'monstrously', 'with a terrible grandeur' – all go far beyond the excesses of Wedekind. Finally there ensues 'terrifying silence'; it follows Mississippi's declaration: 'I have come to ask you to be my wife.' After he has convinced Anastasia he makes a 'terrible' confession of his own: he has killed his wife with the same poison, confiscated from Übelohe, as she was having a cup of coffee after her lunch. But: 'I am not a murderer. Between your deed and mine there is an infinite difference. What *you* did in response to a dreadful impulse *I* did in obedience to a moral judgment. You slaughtered your husband; I executed my wife.' In accordance with the law of Moses, Mississippi punishes his wife for her adultery, and now in order to atone for this breach of modern laws, he condemns himself to marry Anastasia, for whom the marriage is also meant to be a means of atonement. 'Our marriage would mean hell for both parties!' Anastasia, faced with no alternative, consents to this 'martyrdom', which for Mississippi is a 'triumph of justice!'

In a speech to the audience Mississippi tells how his influence during the course of five years purified Anastasia:

> As I had foreseen, my wife's character grew substantially deeper and she even acquired a more positive attitude towards religious sentiments; she watched the executions at my side with perfect calm and composure, without ever losing her natural sympathy with the victims; her daily prison visits which soon became an emotional need for her, continually increased her desire to help, so that she was universally known as the Angel of the Prisons; in short, it was a fruitful period which brilliantly confirmed my thesis that strict laws strictly obeyed are alone capable of making man a better, nay a higher being.

Then follows, forming the substance of the rest of the play, the 'frightful' end of this marriage: the Minister of Justice, an embodiment of pure opportunism and pragmatism (in contrast to the three heroes, each of whom is seeking in his own way to realise an absolute) calls upon Mississippi, in the name of the Government, to retire from his office as Public Prosecutor, because his severity (he has just obtained his three hundred and fiftieth death sentence) is no longer expedient: 'At one moment we have to cut off heads in the name of God, at the next we must be merciful to please the devil; no State can avoid that.' Mississippi rejects the request for his retirement categorically: 'Justice cannot be changed!'

The Minister goes, Saint-Claude comes (the artificiality of this 'relay system', common in drawing-room comedies, is satirised by making the one who has just come on continue smoking the cigar which the one who has just gone off has left in the ashtray) – for the first time Saint-Claude takes part in the action; strangely enough he comes out of Anastasia's room. Equally strangely, he greets Mississippi as a friend whom he has not met for thirty years. The two of them proceed to tell each other what they already know (the animated expressiveness of their dialogue satirises the artificiality of this kind of 'exposition' which is common in drawing-room comedies).

Let us not forget our noble birth. No more than five lire was paid for our begetting; the gutter ran red as we came; rats showed us what life is, their fur wet with sewage; from the vermin that crawled over our bodies we learned how time passes, never to return . . . First we stole the rags that covered our bodies, and filthy copper coins to buy mouldy bread for our bellies; then we were forced to sell ourselves, white victims in the hands of the bourgeois whose cries of pleasure rose to heaven like the miauling of cats; and finally – with violated backsides, but with the pride of young capitalists – we used our hard-earned money to run a brothel, I as the proprietor and you as the doorkeeper.

One of them 'found in the corner of a damp cellar a half-mouldered Bible', and the 'vision of the law' flowed over him 'like a sea of fire': the other found 'Karl Marx's *Kapital* in the pocket of a murdered ponce' and he is overcome by the vision of 'how this world that stinks of hunger, drink and crime could be improved, this hell that resounds with the singing of the rich and the howling of the exploited'. Saint-Claude and Mississippi rose out of the gutter, 'the last two great moralists of our age', and now the Communist calls upon the Public Prosecutor to join him in bringing about a world revolution. In Saint-Claude and Mississippi two conceptions of justice stand irreconcilably opposed.

SAINT-CLAUDE. You want to save an imaginary soul and I a real body!

MISSISSIPPI. There is no justice without God!

SAINT-CLAUDE. There is only justice without God. Nothing can help man but man. But you staked your money on another card – on God. That is why you must now give up the world; if you believe in God man is for ever evil, since goodness rests with God alone . . . what the world needs is not redemption from sin but redemption from hunger and oppression; it has no need to pin its hopes on Heaven, it has everything to hope for from this world.

These arguments leave Mississippi cold; he does not vacate his moralistic position and calmly accepts Saint-Claude's threat to destroy him by revealing his origins to the world. The audience is now given an account of how this is done – by means of headlines, special editions of the newspapers, organised demonstrations – by Übelohe, the wretched doctor who, five years ago – because of an investigation by Mississippi concerning the poison handed over to Anastasia – fled to Borneo, founded a jungle hospital and at this precise moment, bankrupt and worn-out, has returned driven by love for Anastasia. The 'crafty author' he complains, burdened him with 'the curse of a truly ludicrous life and gave

me, not a Beatrice or a Proeza – or whatever lofty being a
Catholic bestows upon his fine, upstanding heroes – but an
Anastasia'. Übelohe is still not allowed to enter the action of
the play (there is something unnerving about the shrewdness
with which Dürrenmatt gives the audience some information
in advance and deliberately witholds other information for
a long time): for our benefit Mississippi performs a scene
which has been omitted, in which he persuades Anastasia to
confess publicly with him, that she has committed murder.
This scene is a parody of Brechtian alienation: both comment
on their actions: 'Deeply moved, I said' . . . 'Thereupon I
kissed his hand' . . . 'And I said in a low voice' . . . A little
later, in a parody of Claudel, three clerics cross the stage and
chant a psalm of praise to Anastasia's virtue.

But, at the beginning of the third 'Act' Anastasia is
wrapped in the arms of Minister of Justice. Outside Saint-
Claude is inciting his followers to lynch Mississippi, yet the
Minister finds that

> it is good to kiss when the world is falling apart, the corpses lie
> like pale flowers amongst the barricades, strewn over carpets
> of crimson. In moments like this it's easy to wax poetical. At one
> time I used to write my poems on white handmade paper; now
> I love to scribble my poems with bloodstained fingers in the
> Book of History.

Übelohe interrupts this idyllic moment, the Minister flees,
Anastasia welcomes the unexpected homecomer as her
saviour. She does not want to stand trial with Mississippi,
but to escape with Übelohe to Chile. 'We don't need much,
Bodo. You're a doctor and I shall give piano lessons.' But
Übelohe has returned in a fanatical search for truth: he intends to admit to Mississippi that Anastasia was his mistress
and murdered her husband so that she could marry him.
Anastasia is trapped, she must wait for her husband with
Übelohe, 'The last champion of faith and hope, in this God-
forsaken room', for the confession of their guilt and their

love is meant to cause a 'miracle' which will save them both.
They wait. Saint-Claude, who is exploiting the uproar over
Mississippi in order to unleash the revolution, and the
Minister, who seizes power amid general chaos, appear
alternately in the windows to make a speech. Mississippi,
hounded by Saint-Claude's mob, bleeding, his clothes in
tatters, staggers into the room. Stones come hurtling in, later
the rattle of machine-gun fire can be heard – slowly the late
bourgeois splendour disintegrates into dust and rubble –
crawling through the barrage Übelohe and Mississippi reach
the middle of the room and meet beneath the Biedermeier
table. And in this half-mad, drunken Don Quixote of charity,
Mississippi recognises the saviour:

MISSISSIPPI. You try in vain to veil your unwordliness in
   a cloak riddled with holes, Count. You cannot hide the scar,
   the fiery mark of Grace in the middle of your heart: it shines
   through your drunkenness and bankruptcy, a red crystal!
ÜBELOHE. So you recognise me?
MISSISSIPPI: I recognise you. There, receive the kiss of Judas!
   I, who judge the world, have renounced you, you who love
   the world. Christendom is dead; the two stone tablets which
   God sundered from Mount Sinai will overturn and bury us.

This bold elevation of the characters takes place only in the
first version of the play. In 1956 Dürrenmatt eliminated almost
all the religious imagery from the text (for example, Anastasia's confession to Übelohe; 'I bleed because I love you.
I love you so much that I dug my nails into my flesh'): this is
the only occasion in Dürrenmatt's work when a new version
means not a clarification, an enlargement of the dimensions,
but a reduction, a toning down. (Of a third, unpublished
version dating from 1959 Dürrenmatt says: 'Out of a more
religiously-angled comedy there grew a political farce'.) In the
text of 1956 there is no kiss of Judas; the great dialogue has
been boiled down to just two lines:

MISSISSIPPI. Are you a Christian?
ÜBELOHE. I am a Christian.

Immediately following this – the revolution outside the windows has ended, with Saint-Claude defeated – Übelohe confesses his love for Anastasia and their adultery five years ago. Mississippi, unswerving in his conviction that he has 'purified' her, fetches his wife and solemnly brings her into the proceedings – and Anastasia swears by God that Übelohe has never touched her. With this the discussion has reached a point where there are no more arguments, where no more dialogue is possible. A grotesque intermezzo must break the tension, clear the stage. The room fills with white-coated psychiatrists, who enter through the doors, the windows and even through the grandfather clock – the whole psychiatric congress, convened by the new Prime Minister to give expert opinion on Mississippi and to commit him to an asylum. The Public Prosecutor screams at them. 'I poisoned my first wife and my second wife poisoned her first husband!' That is all the doctors need in order to declare him insane and to take him away without further ado.

ANASTASIA. The miracle has happened. We are free.
ÜBELOHE. And yet parted.
ANASTASIA. For ever.
ÜBELOHE. Faith is lost. A little water that trickled away into the sand.

Übelohe goes out, the hopeless victim of a hopeless love: 'Thus I have been flung upon a world that is now beyond salvation, / and nailed upon the cross of my absurdity, / I hang upon this beam / that mocks me, / exposed unprotected / to the gaze of God, / a last Christ.'
A monologue by Saint-Claude introduces the last 'Act': he is a failed revolutionary, expelled from the Party, hunted by the police and by his comrades. He comes to Anastasia who thus far has concealed him and with whom he now wants to

flee, in order to begin the world revolution afresh, somewhere else, perhaps in Portugal.

Over a cup of coffee at the Biedermeier table in the middle of the devastated room, he unfolds his plan:

> We'll start in the sewers, rise to the doss-houses, move to the pubs and finally I shall build you a decent brothel . . . In future you will live upon those against whom all revolutions have been directed – the rich. As the Angel of the Prisons you were an insult, in your new employment you will be one of the most natural means of obtaining money from the possessing class which will help you to bring about its downfall.

Anastasia appears to go along with this but simultaneously slips the last dose of her usual poison into his coffee cup. Saint-Claude sees her, drinks the coffee from her cup while she is in her room preparing for the escape; then he leaves to fetch a car.

Meanwhile, Mississippi has escaped from the asylum and reached his room unnoticed. Now he enters, dressed in the ceremonial black robe of the Public Prosecutor, fills Anastasia's coffee cup and puts his last dose of poison into it. Anastasia appears, ready for the escape (this is not consistent with her attempt to poison Saint-Claude: but we accept it as an excuse to bring her on in a flame-red evening dress, appropriate to the solemnity of this final reckoning). Once again, as at the beginning, Anastasia and Mississippi face each other across the Biedermeier table. Each knows that the other's coffee is poisoned – it would hardly be possible to invent a theatrical situation loaded with more *a priori* tension – yet Dürrenmatt does not protract the dénouement: both drink their coffee, both are now certain that the other is about to die. Mississippi ('Madame, I shall now carry out the final interrogation') asks again if she did not swear falsely, yet Anastasia clings to her lie, even when Mississippi tells her she has taken poison and that perjury intensifies her guilt.

Anastasia dies, a monstrous lie on her lips – of course this is highly impressive, but also very odd. Why does she give away her moment of triumph, when she could destroy Mississippi's faith in her and his love by telling the truth; why does she decide not to tell him that she has poisoned him? Without a doubt a final melodramatic revelation would be more effective, maybe even, from the point of view of the characterisation, more plausible. Yet Anastasia refrains from doing so – or rather, Dürrenmatt denies her because he does not want Mississippi's faith to be destroyed. Only the audience is to know how futile his exultation is, how illusory his belief that he has transformed a she-devil into an angel: 'My marriage was a terrible experiment. I fought for the world and won.' Saint-Claude returns to collect Anastasia (incredibly, for after all she had tried to poison him), and, instead of destroying Mississippi's illusion, he patiently listens to the last fantasies of the dying man:

> I shall flee with you, brother . . . We'll found a brothel. I'll be the doorkeeper and you do duty inside. Then if heaven and hell break apart, we shall plant the red flag of Justice in the midst of the tottering edifice of the world.

Mississippi collapses, the three men in raincoats with red armbands, whom we met earlier, enter and shoot Saint-Claude. The play is over.

Three corpses in one scene: this piece of Grand Guignol unmistakably brings the drawing-room drama to an end. But can a comedy of conflicting ideologies to be resolved with bullets and poison? Of all people, it seems to us that Anastasia is the one who ought to be unconquerable, essentially immortal, ineradicable, always having the upper hand: she ought to stride away, arm in arm with the Minister over the corpses, triumphant. A poisoned cup of coffee has robbed Dürren-matt's attempt at a 'Dialectic with characters' of its final consequence. It is logical that the men, although they are only personified ideas, should put the seal on their failure to come to grips with the world by dying a pitiful stage death: but the woman, personification of the world on which their hopes are dashed to pieces, ought not by rights to be allowed to share their trivial fate but ought to be the theatrical victor. The common fate of the characters destroys the distance between the world and the idea.

The epilogue which Dürrenmatt has devised does not re-establish this distance; the corpses get up, Anastasia embraces the Minister who pops up at the window, Saint-Claude and Mississippi sing of the unquenchable yearning for justice which used to possess them and will continue unquenchably to do so: 'Again and again we return, as we have always returned / in ever new shapes, yearning for ever more distant paradises.'

Dürrenmatt tells us that he discovered 'the possibility of a dialectic with characters' in Wedekind's *Marquis of Keith*. There is no doubt that this glorified drawing-room drama, even in the style of its dialogue, is closer to Wedekind than any other of his comedies. The similarity between the first Act of Wedekind's *Wetterstein Castle* and the exposition of *Mississippi*, which, at the première, even gave rise to suspicions of plagiarism, is of course superficial (no stronger than the similarity between the conversation under the Biedermeier table and a scene in O'Casey's *Shadow of a Gunman*).

It is conceivable that the character Effie in *Wetterstein Castle* influenced the figure of Anastasia, for this terrible *femme fatale* is quite unique in Dürrenmatt's theatrical world, which otherwise contains only young heroines with the absoluteness of Kleist's Käthchen von Heilbronn and old ladies with the absoluteness of a stone Nemesis. Anastasia – not a human being but a theatrical monstrosity – might well bear traces of a Wedekind-woman but the type of play Dürrenmatt involves her in is entirely his own, as are her partners, the creatures whose existence she destroys without, being able to destroy their boundless faith.

Extreme idealists engaged in a constant search for absolutes, in other words, potential tragic heroes, who come to a ludicrous end – above all Übelohe, the fool in Christ who, as he says, was cast by Dürrenmatt into the 'crucible of his comedy' to show 'whether in this finite Creation God's mercy is really infinite'. Übelohe, whose greatness is turned into absurdity, 'like a dice which unfathomably, senselessly turns up a one at every throw', has the last word: a Don Quixote in his faith, he staggers across the stage once more towards imaginary windmills, asserting his faith in the absurdity of his own and of all life in a sort of hymn: 'An eternal comedy / Let His glory blaze forth / Fed by our helpless futility.'

6

An Angel Comes to Babylon

This is another play about God's grace and divine justice, but removed from the Christian sphere into an oriental fairy-tale world, which permits a certain theological and theatrical naivety. In it, Heaven can take on a visible theatrical form as a starry celestial back-drop, in the middle of which, 'oppressively close' hovers the gigantic mass of the Andromeda Galaxy; in it the incarnate grace of a God, who is no protestant *deus absconditus* and who by no means leaves his creation to its own devices, can be brought to earth by an Angel: a pure, radiantly beautiful girl by the name of Kurrubi ('cherub') whom God has created out of nothing and whom he has destined to be the bride of the 'lowliest' of men. Babylon, the mythical metropolis, has been furnished by Dürrenmatt with sky-scrapers and a Euphrates waterfront, with streetcars and gas-lamps, in order to emphasise that it is the capital of the world (or at least regards itself as such: for Nebuchadnezzar, as provincial as any of us, does not know that there are a few other villages beyond the Lebanon – Athens, Sparta, Carthage, Moscow, Peking).

When the Angel, disguised as a beggar, enters Babylon with Kurrubi, intent on handing her over to the lowliest of men, Nebuchadnezzar has just conquered his eternal opponent Nimrod and has regained the throne. Since time immemorial the two have reigned alternately over the world, chained to the steadily revolving wheel of History: 'I on top, you beneath, you on top, I beneath, for ever and ever.' During the 900 years that he languished, spat upon by all the courtiers, as a footstool beneath the feet of Nimrod, Nebuchadnezzar has been planning social reforms ('Kings invariably think in socialist terms when they find themselves in a humiliating position'), and his first act has been to prohibit begging. Following his edict all beggars have become civil servants and tax-collectors – all except Akki, whose entire existence is passionately devoted to begging and who lives under one of the bridges which cross the Euphrates, the living essence of anarchy: 'Secret teachers we are, educators of the people. We go in rags as a tribute to man's wretchedness, and we obey no law, that freedom may be held in honour.'

In order to convert this fellow Akki to the new social order 'humanely' (after flogging and torture have achieved nothing), Nebuchadnezzar passes himself off as a beggar and goes to the bank of the Euphrates to meet him. Akki will have nothing at all to do with the advantages of the new State: instead he challenges the king, who has introduced himself as 'Anashamashtaklakou, the great, the famous; out-

standing and supreme among the beggars of Nineveh', to a
begging contest: 'If you win, we'll both enter the State
service at eight in the morning. If I win, we'll both carry on
begging, undisturbed by the dangers which beset our lofty
calling.' This helps the Angel too, who had been thrown right
out of his stride by the appearance of *two* lowliest men; he
concludes: 'Whoever loses this begging match must be the
lowliest of mankind.' The ensuing begging contest is a
theatrical show-piece of the highest order, a scene so in-
telligently conceived and constructed that it alone makes the
beggar Akki into one of the juiciest, most life-like figures not
only in Dürrenmatt's work, but in the entire German theatre of
today (certainly on a par with many a similar Brechtian-figure,
like, for instance, Azdak in *The Caucasian Chalk Circle*).

Akki naturally wins round after round, for he knows how
to aim at his victims' weakest spots: the labourer's working-
class consciousness, the milk merchant's middle-class self-
reliance, the prostitute's social ambitions, the banker's pride.
Nebuchadnezzar has already suffered ignominious defeat
when soldiers drag past the captive Nimrod; and, 'with
sudden inspiration', the king suggests to Akki: 'Whoever can
beg him shall be the winner of our contest.' Akki rubs his
hands: 'Done. A trifling, but attractive little problem in the
art of begging.' Nebuchadnezzar beckons the soldiers to him,
whispers to them that he is the king and asks them to hand
over Nimrod to him. 'Very good, Your Highness,' is the
answer – and the soldiers grin as they knock him to the
ground. Now Akki intervenes: 'Do you know who it is you
have knocked down? . . . You've probably never heard of the
habit kings have of dressing up as beggars and sitting by the
banks of the Euphrates to study how people live.' He pretends to be the Prime Minister, 'likewise dressed as a beggar
and studying the life of the common people'. He has Nimrod
handed over to himself and chases the soldiers away. Nebuchadnezzar's defeat is total. Akki remains a beggar.

c

And now the Angel's moment has arrived: he casts off his disguise, announces the will of God, and hands over Kurrubi to the 'beggar Anashamashtaklakou' and flies off. Kurrubi remains alone with her beggar, to whom she is devoted from now on with undying love; but who is busy quarrelling with God: 'Why doesn't Heaven understand the loneliness of Nebuchadnezzar? Why should you be sent to mock both me, the beggar, and Nebuchadnezzar the King?' He strikes Kurrubi down and finally exchanges her for Nimrod with Akki.

With its gently ironic fairy-tale mood, reminiscent of Giraudoux, full without being heavy, this first Act is beautifully rounded, self-enclosed, and has only one blemish: its conclusiveness. Kurrubi is in fact in the hands of the man for whom Heaven destined her – does not the Angel's mistake really contain truth and is not Nebuchadnezzar, superficially the most magnificent of men, really the lowliest of mankind? But in that case what would Nimrod be? The story is obviously not over with this first Act and yet it contains no motivation for further development of the action. Thus this virtuoso exposition is at the same time a trap in which the play has ensnared itself. Despite his frequent remarkably concentrated attempts to set it free, in the last analysis Dürrenmatt has not succeeded. Perhaps at the decisive moment he was hampered by the conclusion towards which he wished his intractable plot to lead: Nebuchadnezzar resolves to build a tower up to Heaven and gain revenge on God. But the King could have made this plan if the contrasts had been pointed a little more sharply at the end of the first Act when he goes back to his palace 'tired and saddened, insulted by Heaven itself'.

We shall not speculate on how the play might be better developed out of such an ending to the Act, or how it might have turned out in the end if Dürrenmatt had abandoned the idea of the building of a tower – in any case his work began with just this idea, and was to tell the background story of the Tower of Babel. Yet now, despite all the playwright's tricks, the story will no longer grow out of it convincingly. Dürrenmatt's commentary on the 1957 version reads:

> This comedy tries to expound the reason why a tower came to be built in Babylon, which, according to the legend, was to be one of the most grandiose though senseless enterprises mankind has ever attempted; all the more important since we see ourselves today entangled in similar enterprises. My thoughts, my dreams had revolved for years around this theme: even in my youth I had been occupied with it. In my father's library there was a blue and white volume of monographs on world history, Nineveh and Babylon. It is difficult to dramatise dreams. It was never my intention to depict a lost world – I was lured on by the possibility of turning my impressions into my own personal world. The work stretched over years. A serious attempt to put all the Tower material into shape as a play failed in 1948; five years later I tried again, keeping the first Act and changing the plot. Now the subject was to be simply the cause of the building of a tower. Thus a version emerged which was produced first in Munich and then in other cities. It was unsatisfactory. I needed a break, I needed to turn my thoughts to something different, to achieve distance, to shape the comedy dramaturgically from the point of view of production, to let it become action and nothing more. Provided something has a basis of truth then that truth will not fail to manifest itself. I do not know yet whether the plot will be taken any further. According to my plan, the actual building of the Tower is to be represented in my next play: *The Conformers*. Everybody is against the Tower and yet it still gets built . . .

This sounds plausible and also arouses our curiosity (in her study of Dürrenmatt, Elisabeth Brock-Sulzer gives an account of a different plan for the continuation of this theme), yet the sub-title of the 1957 version, 'a fragmentary comedy', lets one suppose that even Dürrenmatt does not consider that the problems of this self-contained play have been conclusively solved. The continuation (written in 1953 and 'reorganised' in 1957) on from the first Act (dating from 1948) leads, after a new start, a change of direction and a final climax, to an end which could already have been reached in the first Act. A comparison between the two versions shows the meaning of the sentence: 'Provided something has a basis of truth then that truth will not fail to manifest itself.' With a few minor insertions and shifts of motive in the second Act, and with a more consistent execution of the third by which Akki gives a plausible function, there emerges from the somewhat arbitrary succession of potentially highly dramatic, 1953-style ideas a carefully woven plot which moves – albeit in a circle – under its own steam.

Akki, whose home is under a bridge over the Euphrates, surrounded by art-treasures from all ages, pestered by fifty poets, whom he sustains, and entertains with (poetically powerfully constructed) sagas of his life – Akki continues to beg in defiance of the royal decree. But his independence is threatened not only by the police (he has even rejected the offer of a high position in the Finance Ministry in order to remain 'an independent artist' and is now under sentence of death), but also, unintentionally, by Kurrubi. Everyone who sees her falls in love with her and starts writing poetry. Suddenly Akki is faced with a whole series of suitors asking for her hand: the labourers, the policeman, the milk merchant, the wine merchant, the banker. Jealous wives intervene and in the midst of all this tumult the Angel appears, singing the praises of the beauty of the earth and of the harmony of the Creation. His entrance changes popular opinion: Kurrubi, unhappily torn between opposing factions, shall belong not to *one* but to *all*, as queen. She is to be brought to Nebuchadnezzar in stormy triumph; Akki, having sadly let her go ('you came to me, a fragment of Heaven, in a chance bargain, and clung to me, like a thread of God's Grace, uncomplaining and cheerful, until another puff of wind has

come to carry you away again'), remains alone with his fifty
lamenting poets.

Then the hangman enters, 'dressed formally in depressing
black. He carries a small suitcase': incorruptibility in person.
Akki invites him to dine, drinks a toast with him to the unchangeable 'bureaucracy, beggary and hanging' (as the hangman says: 'these three are the hidden framework of the
world, within which all else rises and falls'), then lets the
soap-smeared noose be put round his neck without a word
of protest and takes his leave, parodying Hölderlin: 'Whatever's left I bequeath to the Poets. The only puzzle is what
to do with my second-hand bookshop in Flood Street.' This
skilfully calculated twist (Akki knew about the hangman's
passion for books) brings his salvation; Akki trades his life
and the hangman's job for the imaginary second-hand bookshop. He goes off, wearing the hangman's red cloak, consoling
the poets with his 'last and most bitter saga, the saga of the
weapons of the weak'.

In the royal palace, Nebuchadnezzar, grown melancholy
with yearning for Kurrubi, meets the beggar once more:
Akki, unrecognised in the red cloak, announces that begging
has now been stamped out:

NEBUCHADNEZZAR. The Beggar Akki?
AKKI. Transformed. Were he to appear before Your Majesty,
    you would find him unrecognisable.
NEBUCHADNEZZAR. Strung up?
AKKI. He has gone up in the world. He moves now in the
    highest circles.
NEBUCHADNEZZAR. That great patron of the poets will
    hardly have got to Heaven.
AKKI. A little lower than that.

The next stage of Nebuchadnezzar's realisation of his
allegedly socialist, but in fact totalitarian idea of a state is to
'introduce reason'. Unintentionally fanning the flames of the

king's rage against Heaven, Akki advises that Nebuchadnezzar should start by rooting out the theologians. Yet
Utnapishtim, the Senior Theologian, is flexible enough to be
able to twist the meaning of the Divine Will: 'You confused
the Angel, but God, who sent him, knew to whom He was
giving the girl. To you, King Nebuchadnezzar' – and coun-
sels marriage to Kurrubi. The Prime Minister, suspecting
republican revolutionary elements in the people's uprising,
which has meanwhile reached the palace gates, agrees: 'Never
before have events played so positively into our hands. As a
politician I am delighted. We have the chance to use religion
to stabilize a structure which stands on very weak political
foundations.' Kurrubi is brought in and recognises Nebuchadnezzar, but refuses to accept him as a king:

KURRUBI. By the Euphrates you were the man I loved. Now
   you are a ghost who frightens me.
NEBUCHADNEZZAR. You are confusing appearances with
   reality.
KURRUBI. It is only as a beggar that you are real.
NEBUCHADNEZZAR. It is only as a beggar that I am a
   sham.

Utnapishtim intervenes soothingly: 'Men want to see grace
bestowed on their Kings, not on their beggars. They want
to see you as Queen, and not as a poor thing huddled in
rags.' After a long, rather complicated, sometimes confused
discussion (for in the background Nebuchadnezzar is constantly wrestling Nimrod for the possession of the throne and
Akki is off-stage carousing with the people he is supposed to
be hanging), Kurrubi is more or less won for the King; but
that would not fit in with the planned ending, and so the
Prime Minister, who only a few moments before was seeking
a metaphysical foundation for monarchy, asks Kurrubi to
deny the Angel and her divine origins:

A State and sound government are only possible if earth
remains earth and Heaven Heaven; since earth presents reality

which has to be dealt with by politicians, and Heaven is a charming theory of the theologians about which nobody else needs to bother very much. If, however, Heaven becomes a reality, as now through the appearance of the Angel, human order collapses, since, faced by a visible Heaven, the State is inevitably reduced to a farce. And here we have before us the result of this cosmic carelessness: the people have risen against us.

The only way Dürrenmatt can justify this violent volte-face is by having the popular uprising mistaken for a revolution (the aim of which however has just been achieved) and by a feeble joke ('the more often a politician contradicts himself, the greater he is'). With his stated goal always firmly in mind the dramatist adds twist after twist: if nothing else, this third Act is a triumph of artistry over matter. Now the climax, too, is in sight, for Kurrubi cannot be persuaded at any price to acquiesce in the explanation that the angel was one of the Court actors, or in the infamous 'paraphrase of the wonderful truth, for publication to people who will turn anything out of the ordinary into crude sensationalism' (Utnapishtim). She says: 'Your power is weakness ... Your riches are poverty. Your love for me is self-love. You neither live nor are you dead. You exist, but you have no existence. Let me go, King of Babylon, away from you and from this city.'

Nebuchadnezzar admits defeat and grants audience to the 'revolutionaries', who tell him that, 'whereas we wish to have this girl as Queen, we do not absolutely insist on your Majesty as King'. Once again Dürrenmatt has to ward off a possible ending – the victory of this idea. Nebuchadnezzar finds it strangely easy to incite the people against Kurrubi; suddenly she is described as a witch, a bringer of misfortune, misery and death, and is abruptly handed over to the hangman. Even the Angel who at this moment appears once more, praising the earth as a Star of Grace, cannot bring about another shift of opinion. Nebuchadnezzar, almost mad with despair and rage, announces his plan:

> I will herd mankind into one great enclosure and in the midst of it I will raise a tower which shall pierce the clouds and, traversing the infinities of space, reach the very heart of my enemy. I will oppose to the Creation out of the void the creation of the spirit of man, and we shall see which is the better: my justice, or the injustice of God.

Akki and Kurrubi flee away across the desert towards a new land, 'rising in the silver light of a new dawning, full of new persecutions, but full, too, of new promises, and full of the songs of a new morning'.

Dürrenmatt's wish, 'after what was certainly a rather complicated comedy, *The Marriage of Mr Mississippi*', was to write 'something simple', and he undertook the 'attempt to get out of the dramatic cul-de-sac into which *The Marriage of Mr Mississippi* had lured me. The new play was to be self-contained, strictly rectilinear and colourful.' By 'dramatic cul-de-sac' he probably means the excessive shattering of illusions in in *The Marriage of Mr Mississippi*, perhaps also the purely parodistic style of dialogue; but is the new play, because it appears more serious, more honest, more unpretentious, really any simpler? Dürrenmatt's conversion to simplicity (written after the 1953 première) hides a remarkable lack of self-knowledge. For the revolutionary upheavals of the Babylonian comedy create more dramaturgic disarray than Saint-Claude's revolution, and the King's elaborately contrived hubris together with the (in itself quite spiritedly parodied) opportunism of the statesmen and clerics in effect overwhelm the 'strictly rectilinear' design of the plot.

Basically it is a question of a heaven-sent being (like Strindberg's 'Daughter of Indra', in *A Dream Play*), who becomes acquainted with all the distress, sickness, injustice and cruelty of this world, and yet shall not say: 'mankind is to be pitied,' because someone is there who teaches her to love the earth in all its imperfection, because it is the only earth, 'unique in happiness and unique in danger, varied and wild, possessing marvellous possibilities'. Never again has Dürrenmatt so sharply pointed the question of the dichotomy between earthly and heavenly justice as in this play about a gift of God which may not belong to the man who needs it urgently and which is granted to the man who needs it least.

An Angel Comes to Babylon is a 'fragmentary comedy' not because the insoluble question remains unsolved but because the story is not taken to its 'worst possible turning' (which would also answer the question). 'It is difficult to dramatise dreams.'

7
The Visit

The first comedy of Dürrenmatt's to achieve its final form without the need for wholesale revision, to take a single dominant idea to its ultimate conclusion without the slightest digression is *The Visit*. This is not only his most successful but also his best play, the one which most clearly demonstrates the characteristic qualities of his dramatic style and the one which most simply allows a bitter worldliness to speak out via the plot, of its own accord, without the aid of rhetorical explications. The idea on which it is based is grandiose.

Claire Zachanassian, the richest woman in the world, pays a return visit to Guellen, the small town where she spent her youth, and which forty-five years earlier she had left as the poverty-stricken Clara Wascher. She receives a rapturous welcome, for it is hoped that the famous benefactress will come to the aid of her utterly run-down and impoverished home town. Claire Zachanassian is willing to do so to a staggering extent: 'Five hundred thousand for the town and five hundred thousand to be shared among each family.' True, but 'on one condition . . . I'm giving you a million and I'm buying myself justice'. Forty-five years ago Clarie Wascher was betrayed by her lover Alfred Ill, made to seem untrustworthy by bribed witnesses in a paternity suit and hounded in shame from the town. Now she has returned as Claire Zachanassian and she demands justice. 'I can afford it. A million for Guellen if somebody kills Alfred Ill.'

Using the framework of a well-tried method of exposition, the comedy begins with the announcement of, and contrived preparations for, the visit: the inquisitiveness of the waiting Guelleners is irresistibly transferred to the audience. Dürrenmatt uses the conventional opening of the play not only to establish with concise, extremely clear strokes the pitiable condition of the town of Guellen but also to put us in the position of the Guelleners: like them we await the visit, like them we are astonished and fascinated by the old lady's pompous arrival: like them we react with spontaneous indignation to her outrageous demand for revenge. Dürrenmatt ('who is not so sure, whether he would have acted differently') guides us into solidarity with the Guelleners, which we cannot simply renounce when we see that she corrupts them into criminal complicity. The method which as it were turns the audience into Guelleners is effective even in the first scene: for it shows us four spectators who are sitting on a bench outside the local station, watching the express trains roaring past, discussing the great event that is soon to occur and the hopes which they have of it.

In four sets of four impersonally lapidary statements they

express all there is to say about the deterioration of the town:
'Ruined – The Wagner factory gone crash – Bockmann bankrupt – The Foundry on Sunshine Square shut down – Living
on the dole – On Poor Relief soup – Living? Vegetating –
And rotting to death – The entire township.' The ringing of
the station bell acts as a caesura, a change of theme ensues;
after a further four sentences we know all about the expected
visit:

> It's more than time that millionairess got here. They say she
> founded a hospital in Kalberstadt . . . She and her money. She
> owns Armenian Oil, Western Railways, North Broadcasting
> Company and the Hong Kong – uh – Amusement District.'

Another acoustic caesura (clatter of a passing train), then
eight elegaic sentences about the former glory of Guellen
('We were a city of the Arts, then . . . Goethe spent a night
here . . . Brahms composed a quartet here'): thus we have all
the relevant information. The preparations for the reception
could begin. However, a bailiff from the capital arrives to
distrain on the entire town of Guellen and to investigate how,
whilst the rest of the country is booming, this place could
have become so wretchedly impoverished. 'We're up against
a real economic enigma,' declares the Mayor. (The solution
to the enigma is not revealed until the third Act: the old Lady
has used intermediaries to buy up the whole town bit by bit
and has systematically 'starved' it – thus in this play the
circle of cause and effect is drawn conclusively and thus
Guellen becomes the perfect example of the total venality
and corruptibility of the world.)

For the present, however, the mood is of untroubled and
pleasurable anticipation. Mayor, Priest, and Schoolmaster
prepare the reception with provincial pomp: speeches, choral
singing, bell-ringing, brass band music, 'the Athletic Club
will honour the millionairess with a pyramid. Then a meal
in the Golden Apostle.' Silently and totally disregarded by

the others Ill has joined the group; now – after an exchange of words which unmistakably testifies to the omnipotence of the earthly bringer of salvation, Claire Zachanassian – he is drawn into the spotlight

MAYOR. Gentleman, the millionairess is our only hope.

PRIEST. Apart from God.

MAYOR. Apart from God.

SCHOOLMASTER. But God won't pay.

MAYOR. You used to be a friend of hers, Ill, so now it all depends on you.

PRIEST. But their ways parted. I heard some story about it – have you no confession to make to your Priest?

ILL. We were the best of friends. Young and hotheaded. I used to be a bit of a lad, gentlemen, forty-five years ago. And she, Clara, I can see her still: coming towards me through the shadows in Petersens' Barn, all aglow. Or walking barefoot in the Konrad's Village Wood, over the moss and the leaves, with her red hair streaming out, slim and supple as a willow, and tender, ah, what a devilish beautiful little witch. Life tore us apart. Life. That's the way it is.

Ill knows what is expected of him – ('Zachanassian has to cough up her millions') and he knows that it depends on the success of his 'mission' whether or not he becomes the Mayor's successor. Already puffed up with his own importance, he declares: 'We've got to be clever, psychologically acute.' Thus the positions are established, the audience carefully prepared for the grand arrival. Of course, the Guelleners are not prepared – but what dramatist could resist the temptation to let such a grandiose visit burst right into the middle of the preparations, causing chaotic disarray? The roar of the oncoming Venice–Stockholm express is followed by the screech of emergency brakes and the train stops: 'It's against the Laws of Nature.'

Enter Claire Zachanassian 'Sixty-three, red hair, pearl necklace, enormous gold bangles, unbelievably got up to kill yet by the same token a Society Lady with a rare grace, in spite of all the grotesquerie'. She is followed by Boby (the eighty-year-old butler), Moby (Husband VII), Roby and Toby (herculean sedan-bearers, gum-chewing monsters, ex-gangsters), with them an entourage of maids and servants, a panther, a black luxury coffin, and, bringing up the rear, Koby and Loby (two blind eunuchs, hand in hand, who always speak in unison). This ostentatious, circus-style entry contrasts harshly and horribly with the embarrassed solemnity of the Guelleners: a world of resounding monumentality has broken into their shabby mediocrity.

The way the millionairess talks is just as inappropriately pompous as her entrance, at once vulgar and pathetic: according to her, trains do not merely go, but 'puff' or 'roar'; she congratulates the Mayor on his 'brats'; she calls upon the Schoolmaster, 'and lover of the noblest Muse', to 'Fire away, Schoolmaster, let's hear your homely folk-song!' Before the song, however, and after the ticket inspector has been pacified with a few thousand and the Mayor has delivered his speech of welcome, Ill timidly steps forward to meet his beloved Clara. With trilling sentimentality she helps him over the initial embarrassment: 'They were wonderful, all those days we used to spend together.' (And Ill whispers to the Schoolmaster standing nearby: 'See, Professor, I've got her in the bag.') Yet the touching duet of reminiscence takes a grotesquely disillusioning turn:

CLAIRE ZACHANASSIAN. I used to call you my black panther.
ILL. I still am.
CLAIRE. Rubbish. You've grown fat. And grey. And drink-sodden.
ILL. But *you're* still the same, my little sorceress.
CLAIRE. Don't be daft. I've grown old and fat as well. And lost my left leg. An automobile accident. Now I only travel in express trains. But they made a splendid job of the artificial one, don't you think?

The old lady – she can afford it – is given to outrageous and
macabre jokes: 'Can you wink a blind eye to things from time
to time?' she asks the Policeman; 'Do you comfort the dying?'
she asks the Priest. Later she asks the Doctor: 'Do you make
out Death Certificates?' and the Gymnast: 'Ever used your
strength for strangling?' Ill, simple, rather obsequious and
jovial, cannot be shaken out of his composure: 'Claire has
such a golden sense of humour! I could die laughing at her
jokes!' But the Schoolmaster, proudly displaying his scholar-
ship, feels the eerie draught blowing from Hades: 'That old
lady in black robes getting off the train was a gruesome
vision. Like one of the Fates; she made me think of an
avenging Greek goddess. Her name shouldn't be Claire;
it should be Clotho. I could suspect her of spinning destiny's webs herself. . . . Gentlemen: I'm stirred. I feel the
grandeur of antiquity in Guellen. I've never sensed it here
before.'

Yet before this antique grandeur reveals itself in all its
gruesomeness, an idyllic scene is played out in the Konrad's
Village Wood. Claire and Ill visit the memorable places of
their youth: the heart with the initials which he once carved
into a tree, the beech tree beneath which they made love,
'among these toadstools on the moss'. Ill tells altruistic lies
('I wanted you to be happy. So I had to renounce being
happy myself') and his words become laden with pathos: 'I've
been living in hell since you went away from me.' Claire
replies: 'And I've grown into hell itself.' But he takes no
notice and slaps her cheerfully on the thigh, as she promises
him a million for Guellen. The blow hurts ('You hit one of
the straps for my artificial leg'), but nevertheless Ill waxes
poetic: 'Now it's the way it used to be when we were young
and bold, when we went out walking in Konrad's Village
Wood, in the days of our young love. The sun was a dazzling
orb, above the pine-trees. And far away a few wisps of cloud,
and somewhere in the woodland you could hear a cuckoo

calling –' and kisses her hand: 'The same, cool white hand –'
'No, you're wrong. It's artificial, too. Ivory.'

Ill's clumsy attempt to ingratiate himself with her (his
'psychologically acute' approach) is tasteless. The exaggeratedly sloppy as well as macabre language lends a lurid theatricality, almost operatic in its effect. Dürrenmatt employs a
supplementary device to break the agony of the situation:
four Guelleners ('We are pines, fires, beeches') simulate trees,
with outstretched arms and twigs in their hands. One of
them springs off: 'Look, a doe,' says Claire; Ill remarks: 'It's
the close season.' The ambivalence of such a reply (for only
too soon is the hunting of Ill to commence) is considerably
more subtle than the business with the doe and the trees, the
entertainment value of which threatens the audacious design
and style of this conversation and almost renders it harmless
by being too comical. Dürrenmatt has defended this device
(which not all directors have used in their productions) with
almost excessive zeal: as a matter of fact this use of 'Chinese'
methods is neither anti-illusionism à la Thornton Wilder nor
Brechtian alienation, but a rather odd attempt to undermine
the desired and necessary effect of the scene as it progresses.
But Dürrenmatt has not undertaken anything similar in any
later play.

The first Act ends with a banquet which the old lady turns
into a trial. Claire counters the Mayor's hypocritical cere-
moniousness with sarcasm; she then reveals her plan for 'an
absolute revenge which is as logical as the laws of primeval
times' (Dürrenmatt). The butler Boby steps forward and
reveals himself as the judge who, forty-five years ago, dis-
missed Clara Wascher's paternity suit against Ill; he recalls
the two witnesses whom Ill had bribed at the time with a
litre of schnaps to swear falsely that they had slept with
Clara – these are Koby and Loby, tracked down by Claire in
Canada and Australia and castrated and blinded as a punishment for their perjury. Now Claire demands that the wrong

verdict be annulled and changed to a sentence of death on Ill
(for even the child died because of him, and Claire became a
prostitute). Ill gets angry: 'It's over and done with, dead and
buried! It's an old crazy story . . . Life went on!' Claire is
immovable: 'You chose your life but you forced me into
mine. A moment ago you wanted time turned back, in that
wood so full of the past, where we spent our young years.
Well, I'm turning it back now, and I want justice. Justice for a
million.' And when the Mayor angrily rejects her demand 'in
the name of humanity', she replies, certain of victory: 'I'll wait.'

The Visit, despite the predominantly sceptical reviews of
the première, has become Dürrenmatt's least disputed world-
wide success, thanks not only to the powerfully contrived
plot, but even more to the 'star' rôle of Claire Zachanassian
which the *monstres sacrés* everywhere thronged to play. This
is surprising for the old lady is certainly not a 'great' rôle,
not one which permits a virtuosa to demonstrate the whole
range of her talents (as does Giraudoux's Madwoman of
Chaillot). This redheaded mummy, dripping with pearls
requires and allows only a single tone: petrified monumentality, coldness (even when she is displaying humour), and
infinite distance. Her dominating effect is due entirely to the
theatrical aplomb with which Dürrenmatt creates her scenes,
the way, for instance, in which he places her throughout the
second Act above the stage on a hotel balcony. What she
actually has to say is grotesque: ('Boby, pass me my left leg')
or pathetic (reminiscences of her earlier marriages: Husband
VII has gone abroad; her wedding with Number VIII is
being prepared in Guellen Cathedral), and in the end irrele-
vant, effective only as a foil for the main action. Yet simply
by her constant presence the old lady demonstrates – more
emphatically than she could do rhetorically – that she is the
authority governing the incidents taking place beneath her
feet: she sits enthroned as a terrible goddess of justice over
Guellen.

What is happening in this scene – the slow change of atmosphere – is pure *reaction*, more or less undramatic, a process which Dürrenmatt cannot rush through with striking suddenness, but must bring about slowly, step by step. The manner of this demonstration aligns the play more closely with Brecht. The gradual corrupting of the Guelleners reveals itself spectacularly in their changing purchasing habits. People are speculating – at first still unconsciously – on Ill's death, on future wealth. They incur debts – the high moral justification of this self-indulgence is supplied later, when they are sated (and it is too late to do anything about it). Guellen begins to flourish, the sales increase, even in Ill's general store: everybody buys creamier milk, more expensive cigarettes, chocolate, cognac – Ill gives credit, proud of the Guelleners' solidarity ('All for one, one for all') and derives reassurance from the fact that he will be elected Mayor in the spring: 'Dead certain Mr Ill, dead certain.' But then he discovers that they are all wearing new shoes – and it dawns on him, perhaps even before they realise it themselves, just what game is being played. He goes to the police and demands that Claire be arrested. They laugh at him: the old lady's demand cannot be taken seriously 'because one million is an exorbitant price, you have to admit that yourself. People offer a hundred, or maybe two hundred, for a job like that, not a penny more, you can bet your life on it.'

A dramatist like Brecht would have concentrated completely on this development of motives (the way morality depends on economic factors): Dürrenmatt's theatrical temperament seeks stronger effects. His development of the plot is rational but to increase its theatricality he uses irrational incidents. Thus Claire's panther (the incarnation of the pet-name which she once gave to Ill) now escapes, which causes great unrest and gives everybody the right to creep around with loaded guns. There is a note of helplessness in Ill's cry of 'It's me you're hunting down, me.' Even the Mayor, with his new shoes and silk tie, can only offer him empty phrases: 'You're forgetting you're in Guellen. A city of Humanist traditions. Goethe spent a night here. Brahms composed a quartet here.' But he is the first to show how people adapt their morality to the economic situation: 'The fact that we condemn the lady's proposal does not mean we condone the crime which led to that proposal. The post of Mayor requires certain guarantees of good moral character which you can no longer furnish. You must realise that.'

'Small towns like this get me down. I know the lime tree's rustling, the birds are singing, the fountain's plashing, but they were all doing all that half an hour ago. And nothing else is happening at all, either to the landscape or to the people, it's all a picture of deep, carefree peace and contentment and cosy comfort. No grandeur, no tragedy. Not a trace of the spiritual dedication of a great age,' says Husband VIII on the hotel balcony to his wife Claire, as Ill crosses the square and goes into the sacristy. 'The town's getting ready to celebrate my murder, and I'm dying of terror.' The Priest fobs him off with fine phrases: 'All they're doing is affirming life, that's all they're doing, affirming life' – then a newly purchased bell begins to toll. 'You too, Father! You too!' cries Ill; and whilst the sound of gunfire can be heard outside (the panther is killed outside Ill's shop), the Priest beseeches him: 'Flee! We are all weak, believers and unbelievers. Flee! The Guellen bells are tolling, tolling for treachery. Flee! Lead us not into temptation with your presence.'

Theatrical analogies, symmetries, reversals all go to make up the structure of Dürrenmatt's plays. This is true in this play: from the single sentence, scarcely noticed, through the coarse comedy of the twin eunuchs, to the overall structure – the railway station at beginning and end, the two meetings between Ill and Claire in the wood, the two court scenes, and, at the end of the Second Act, Ill's attempt to escape, the scenic arrangement of which is repeated with different emotions when he dies. Ill stands at the station, a small suit-case in his hand, resolved to flee, although everybody accom-panies him and declares with one voice, in the friendliest of terms, that he would be safest if he stayed with them. They do not stop him, on the contrary, they wish him, with one voice, in the friendliest of terms, 'An enjoyable trip!' – yet they stand around him like a wall. Ill, paralysed with fear, is incap-able of boarding the waiting train, and when the train leaves, he collapses: 'I am lost.'

In the third Act, Ill conquers his fear, acknowledges the old, unexpiated guilt and faces death with courage. This transformation, this 'breakthrough into greatness', plausible from the point of view of characterisation and necessary for the final turning-point of the drama (so that Ill becomes the antithesis of the Guelleners), cannot be made obvious on stage, because this lonely victory could not be portrayed in dialogue (for which he lacks a suitable partner) and a soliloquy would break the style of the play. Dürrenmatt himself directed a workshop-theatre version of *The Visit* in Bern in 1959 (in four Acts with only twelve actors) and he added a scene in which Ill appears before the old lady on the balcony, falls to his knees and begs for mercy – but even that hardly removes any of the suddenness from the transformation. We learn that Ill has paced up and down in his room all day long; then he emerges, enlightened, courageous and prepared for death. His shop is now gleaming resplendently in its new opulence. Even his wife and children are enjoying the boom without inhibitions and, for the benefit of the journalists who have been enticed to Guellen for Claire's eighth wed-ding, they demonstrate the happiness of a devoted family. For a moment the action falters and the underlying reality is unmasked in broad effects: 'Money alone makes no one happy,' chants Mrs Ill; her husband is photographed as he presses an axe into the Butcher's hand; the Schoolmaster makes one last attempt 'in a resounding voice', to make known the truth but Ill himself silences him. It is all an excess of contrived theatricality to provide a framework for Ill's soft, dispassionate confession: 'I'm not fighting any more . . . That's all my fault, really . . . I can't help myself and I can't help any of you, any more.'

Ill rejects the Mayor's point-blank demand that he should 'as a man of honour, draw your own conclusion' and commit suicide: 'You *must* judge me now. I shall accept your judgment, whatever it may be. For me, it will be justice; what it will be for you, I do not know. God grant you find your judgment justified.' Dürrenmatt does not say explicitly which change of position has been completed here, but the pitiless tone of these words makes it fairly easy to guess: Ill has become the judge of Guellen. By his death, which atones only for his own sin against Claire but not for the treachery of the Guelleners against him, he is condemning his fellow-citizens, burdening them with an inexpiable guilt.

With a ride in his son's car (bought on credit: the father guarantees and pays for it with his life) Ill takes his leave of the world – once again prosperity is caricatured with a light hand, once again, a few Guelleners mime 'Firs, beeches, woodpeckers and cuckoos': in Konrad's Village Wood, Ill again encounters Claire (accompanied by Husband IX.) Now there is no cheap sentimentality, no pathos in Ill's words. Without nostalgia he looks back on his squandered life and does not flinch when Claire tells him: 'Your love died many years ago. But my love could not die. Neither could it live. It grew into an evil thing, like me, like the pallid mushrooms in this wood, and the blind, twisted features of the roots, all overgrown by my golden millions . . . You are in their toils now, and you are lost' – and he goes with a simple 'Goodbye, Clara.'

There follows Ill's condemnation. In a different, 'more realistic' way than in the woodland scenes, but resorting no less to extremes, Dürrenmatt again builds up a background setting deliberately destructive of atmosphere: Radio and newsreel reporters have rushed to Guellen in order to let the whole world take part in the citizens' debate on the 'Claire Zachanassian Endowment'. The pressmen have not the slightest notion of what it is all really about and talk of 'one of the greatest social experiments of the age'. Because of this framework the spectator is once again urged to see things from the Guelleners' point of view; he belongs to the 'insiders', he knows the facts (and must also be present at the execution which follows). At the same time, the hubbub caused by the press compels the Guelleners to dramatise the issue. They put themselves on show, they perform (on a stage on the stage) a travesty of the famous Rütli Oath, the falseness of which is revealed by their ability to repeat it all instantly (because a newsreel camera jams). The increasing prosperity and the increasing demoralisation of the Guelleners are not only apparent in their dress but also in the way they talk: they become more and more solemn, more and more theatrical and eventually express themselves only in rhythmic choruses.

> We are not moved by the money (*huge applause*), we are not moved by ambitious thoughts of prosperity and good living, and luxury: we are moved by this matter of justice and the problem of how to apply it. Nor yet by justice alone but also by all those ideals, for which our forebears lived and fought and for which they died: and which constitute the values of our Western World. (*Huge applause*.)

With this booming rhetoric the Schoolmaster (the last to succumb to temptation) now argues his plea for Ill's murder.

> Now, in God's name, we must take our ideals seriously, even unto death. (*Huge applause*.) For what would be the sense of wealth which created not a wealth of grace? Yet grace can only be accorded to those who hunger after grace. People of Guellen, do you have that hunger? Or is all your hunger common hunger, physical and profane?

Where a crime is so cloaked in the salvationist phraseology of Western Christianity, it is easy for even the most hesitant sinner to take his ideals seriously 'even unto death': The 'Endowment' is accepted unanimously 'not for the sake of the money', as the Guelleners state in chorus, 'but for the sake of justice'.

Then the press is invited to go out for refreshment: we are alone with ourselves. Ill is allowed to smoke one last cigarette (they can now afford courtesy); the Priest wants to pray for him. 'Pray for Guellen' retorts Ill, then he stands up and walks courageously into the lane which the Guelleners have formed – Silence, moonlight: the scene is at once self-sacrifice and profane ritual murder. A knot of men closes silently, then, the lights go up and the knot unties itself: Ill is lying on the floor. 'Heart attack' is the Doctor's diagnosis. 'Died of joy', declares the Mayor to the reassembled journalists. Claire Zachanassian appears, orders the carrying away of the corpse ('Now he looks the way he was, a long while ago: the black panther'), to the mausoleum on the Isle of Capri which has been set aside for him for ages, and hands the Mayor a cheque for a million.

The concluding tableau, 'The Universal Happy-Ending', an ironic apotheosis of prosperity, unites the Guelleners, clad in evening gowns and dress-suits at the station outside their city, 'a flashy incarnation of the up-to-the-minute technics'. As the lady 'immobile . . . like an old stone idol' disappears in her sedan-chair, followed by the coffin containing Ill's body, the choruses of the Guelleners praise their wealth in the style of the Greek tragedies:

Many the monstrous things on earth . . . yet these monstrous things do not exceed the monstrous plight of poverty . . . Now God be praised, for kindly fate has changed all that. . . . Now let us pray to God to protect us all in these hustling, booming, prosperous times; protect all our sacred possessions, protect our peace and our freedom.

The extraordinary, irresistible effect of this play resides –
over and above its theatrical richness and attractiveness – in
three things: it brings to the stage a world which can be
surveyed in its hierarchical order and represented by types
and which is unmistakably our own; it tells a story in which
the moral and dramatic positions coincide perfectly: it ends in
total victory for evil earthly justice: everyone gets what he
deserves.

8

Frank V

Dürrenmatt's theatre is elemental, determined at the outset
by the most primitive form of all drama; on the one hand the
antithetical dialogue between protagonist and antagonist; on
the other hand the tirade, or rhetorical self-presentation of a
character (or occasionally, of several, who are not in opposition to each other but speak with one voice and can therefore
express themselves in chorus). Already in *It is Written*, we see
this *operatic* style fully developed; the play unfolds in spoken
arias, duets, antiphons. In the plays that follow we see the
reintroduction of the 'big speech' (not to be confused with the
monologue, a method of expressing inner action, which
Dürrenmatt has scarcely ever used), and, where it does not
take the form of direct address to the audience, it is 'legiti-
mised' by planting listeners on stage. This penchant for the
tirade (which, he says, is 'more effective than any other
artistic method of getting across the footlights') and for
rhetorical climaxes in which 'the characters are completely

transmuted into language', was bound at some time to lead
Dürrenmatt to opera. Saint-Claude's song, the clerics' trio
and Übelohe's final aria in *The Marriage of Mr Mississippi*
indicate that he was moving in that direction, not to mention
the Angel's hymns and Akki's sagas in *An Angel Comes to
Babylon*, and the choruses in *The Visit* (Dürrenmatt considered
for a long time whether or not he should turn this finale into
an operatic parody).

Frank V is an opera (for actors, of course); the dialogue
continually bursts into song; the chanson can portray the
'utmost potential', the 'concentrated essence' of a character
(and therefore has a significantly different function from that
of Nestroy's couplets or Brecht's songs). The music fulfils
another task (comparable to that which the Guelleners under-
take in the woodland scenes in *The Visit*); it dematerialises
the often agonising, gruesome speeches, raises them to the
level of pure theatricality. Paul Burkhard's melodies are
simple, appealing, occasionally even cheerful and sentimental,
but always appropriate to the effect of the scene.

Despite such an arresting theatrical conception *Frank V*
is not a success. A handful of occasionally attractive ideas for
scenes were set to music, and around them Dürrenmatt constructed and wrote an action, in which – almost inevitably in
view of the chosen approach – various themes and plots
cross and recross without merging with each other. Dürrenmatt's story is of a bank run by gangsters, whose the
proud boast is: 'Never was an honest deal transacted and
never was money paid back.' A series of scenes serves to
demonstrate criminal practices; 'the ingenious, really well
thought-out transactions' cannot be expressed in theatrical
terms: the personnel manager explains that they are 'unfortunately bound by certain dramatic laws', for 'only what
is happening now works on stage'. So we see 'secondary
activities', which can be surveyed; the bank's resident whore
Frieda is set to work on a client to whom money had to be

paid out under pressure. A watch manufacturer is sold a worthless mine on the pretext that it contains uranium. The proprietress of a hotel which is not paying its way is tricked into taking out a fire insurance with the bank by a disguised bank-gangster's promise to see to the prompt burning down of the hotel; the plan is then to reveal the arson and black-mail the lady.

All three deals misfire; two because of the effective inter-vention of events beyond their control – uranium is actually found in the mine and the hotel burns down quite legally having been struck three times by lightning – the third because of human frailty; Frieda takes pity on the client and lets him keep half of his money. The intervention of blind fate in the otherwise completely self-enclosed world of the play remains incomprehensible (pure theatrical magic, used solely for effect); on the other hand Frieda's weakness is typical of the inner constitution of the firm. All the bank-gangsters – with the exception of the directress Ottilie and the personnel manager Egli – suffer from a profound yearning for goodness, decency, humanity. In songs of complaint they speak in turn of their sad fate in having to be criminals, in turn they wail to each other about what they have suffered for their bank, in turn – in the intervals between work – they tell each other stories of honourable men and lament in chorus; 'Decency, decency / Dream of Life / We wait in vain for you.' Each has his yearnings (a cottage in the country, a devoted family, the peace of a prison cell), a sadly demoralised gang indeed, whom the hard-boiled personnel manager, Egli, has re-peatedly to call to order: 'Remember, your sense of duty, you rogues! Where's your spirit of comradeship, you scroundrels? Face up to your responsibilities, you murderers! Or I'll blow you all to smithereens!'

The weakest of all is Frank V, the boss, ('I am not a bank director, I am unfortunately a thoroughly good man'), fond of Goethe and Mörike, an aesthete, degenerate descendant of

monumental bank-gangsters, of whose unscrupulousness he
sings longingly. His own weakness distresses him compared
with his employees, whose inclination towards decency is a
witty reversal of the ordinary man's yearning for 'adventure'
(which is perhaps fulfilled by reading crime stories). He would
prefer to be a cold-blooded big-time gangster, a 'hero' in his
father's mould. The only dare-devil of this type is Richard
Egli, the last indestructible rogue with any real passion for
life in him amongst a gang of smart-alec milksops. With a
staff like this the Frank Bank can no longer flourish and is so
deeply in debt that Frank has decided to dissolve the whole
firm. One after the other, they are supposed to be murdered
or to disappear (the reserves salted away will allow the evening of their lives to be restfully quiet): the creditors will be
left out in the cold. Frank himself starts the process by
faking his own death and withdrawing to a hiding place
which he only leaves in the disguise of a priest.

Thus the liquidation of the bank, as a second theme, is a
demonstration of business practices. The demonstration is
motivated by the taking on of a newcomer into the gang.
The finer points of crime must be explained to him. This addition to the staff (later a second generation whore is to be
engaged) is difficult to reconcile with the simultaneous process of liquidation. Two themes stand in mutual opposition.
It is the same with the liquidation itself: it is motivated simultaneously from within and without, at one moment it is
because the staff have gone soft, at another it is because the
times have made gangsterism in the style of Frank's fore-
fathers too old-fashioned. The whole world has so degener-
ated into legal criminality that honest-to-goodness roguery
is no longer able to compete. 'All around us we see nothing
but the purest, most inhuman honesty,' moans the chief
clerk. And, according to the personnel manager:

What is now merely disgraceful will become insufferable
Through those who after us are conceived in the whores' bed

Of time, wild and greasy.
With us the world of swindling and usury
Is charging headlong, irresistibly into ruin
We are the last rogues in the world
After us only desolate, evil honesty.
Therefore
O public
Rejoice in us whilst we are still on earth . . .
. . . Unbroken, though we may be smashed into a thousand
      pieces
A relic, like you, of a better, more beautiful world
Fearfully we stand before you
Hangmen indeed yet purest Gods
No less great and bloody
Than the heroes of Shakespeare.

The firm of Frank (Dürrenmatt: 'a fictitious model of possible human relationships') does not therefore, despite numerous indications, represent bourgeois capitalism but a counter-world with a counter-morality, which disintegrates partly for psychological reasons (the demoralisation of the gangsters), partly for historical reasons, but finally also for 'metaphysical' ones; the 'Principle of Evil' upon which the counter-morality of the firm was based is refuted by a dying man:

> What we swindle and snatch
> What we blackmail and forge
> Murder, defraud and cheat
> Usure, steal, fence, lie
> We do only because we must.

This is the justification of the gangsters: a resigned confession to the compulsion of evil, the alternative to which, freedom, remains unattainable;

> Freedom is fine, alas, we all know it,
> Yet if you attempt to seize it, it vanishes in a trice.
> The man who is in clover is in a trap,
> And if you want to get out, the trap snaps shut.

The chief clerk Böckmann destroys this conviction in the central scene of the play, the only one which is unreservedly 'heroic'. He lies dying, calls for a priest (his request is refused because he might be tempted to betray the others), Ottilie 'puts him out of his misery' with a lethal injection, and Frank, disguised as a priest, sings a blasphemous chorale. Then Böckmann despairingly reproaches him;

> You think your garb is necessary, like all our crimes. Nothing was necessary, false priest, not the most insignificant fraud, not one single murder . . . At any time we could have changed our ways, at any moment in our evil lives. There is no heritage which couldn't have been eradicated, and no crime which has to be committed. We were free, false priest, created in freedom and abandoned to freedom.

This scene – 'the man for whom the spirit is a means of enjoyment meets the man who in despair is seeking the spirit' – is one of the boldest and most powerful of Dürrenmatt's theatrical moments, yet it is in a play whose very nature condemns it to ineffectiveness and on whose tangle of themes it is unable to impose any order. In fact Ottilie, the stone-hearted beast, introduces – in the penultimate conversation with Böckmann – another, quite personal reason for their unscrupulousness: their children who, having no inkling of the world of their parents, are being educated in Oxford and Montreux. 'I am lost, I am cursed, let God deal with me as he will, but my children must not have to live as I have done; they are to be allowed to be decent people, pleasing God and man.'

Into the Shakespearean story of the gangster-bank there bursts a Shavian domestic drama, for the children 'naturally' are not like the image which Ottilie has of them. Dancing on their ancestors' graves, they introduce themselves with a cynicism beside which all the professional blackguards look like mere naughty children:

We are coming, the young ones who
Slipped out from between your women's legs.
When God saw us he took to his heels.
The devil cries; What on earth is wrong?
We topple your Babylon
Erect our own temple.
The daughter's a whore, the son
Is a warning to his father.
What you didn't drive away long ago
Is now here to drive you away, you dears
. . . Those who begot us didn't get far.
You saw the scandal.
Therefore the young generation,
The two of us,
Will smash the lot away.

Franziska, having absconded from the boarding school in
Montreux, gets herself taken on by Egli as the new resident
whore (after a touching farewell duet, Egli has shot his
fiancée Frieda, who was growing rebellious after twenty
years' service). Herbert, home from Oxford, proclaims himself a blackmailer and then appears when the last four
gangsters, holding each other stalemated with the aid of
machine guns in front of the great safe, are about to wind up
the company:

I am sorry, Dad, . . . your crime was that you wanted to liquidate our ancestral bank, instead of running it differently. All due
respect to our gangster-bank, but its methods are pointless
unless they make a profit. This was no longer the case, so they
should have been changed. That's what you failed to do, Dad.
Because your character is weak. Honesty is not a matter of personality but of organisation. To be honest requires a far greater
lack of consideration than to be evil; only real scoundrels are
able to do what is good. Had you been such a scoundrel, had
you done business legally and with brutal honesty, we would
still be up there amongst the big banks.

Frank V resigns, Herbert becomes Frank VI and takes control, in order to rescue the hidebound firm by opportune use of 'brutal honesty'. In the version of the play first performed in Zürich, Frank V and Ottilie ended up as tramps, Egli as a road-sweeper; the second version of the ending, first performed in Munich, differentiates their fates: Egli enters into service under Herbert, Frank V is locked in the safe and left to die of hunger, but Ottilie is pardoned by her children.

She in the meantime, having had a change of heart as a result of her meeting with her daughter, has tried to have the whole gang blown up. She has made a full confession to the blind, eighty-three-year-old President Traugott von Friedemann [literally 'Trust-God of Man-of-Peace']. 'I demand punishment, Your Excellency. Justice, even if it destroys me.' But Friedemann, believing that 'only trivialities admit of intervention: what you have done however is on a grandiose scale. The world economy would totter if I interfered,' has replied: 'You must not expect a trial, nor justice, nor punishment; they would be too warm and humane for the icy world of honesty into which I now cast you. Expect only mercy.' He hands her a cheque for a million. In the Munich version she joins with her children in a final chorus;

> The ice-world is coming. The glacier is overtaking
> Humanity, which is paralysed and can no longer flee.
> The spirit sought us, it changed.
> We are now iced up in rotten mercy.
> Neither the punishment nor the trial took place,
> And justice was not profitable.

In the later (Munich) version, Ottilie asks the children to kill her, but instead they praise her: 'You were simply marvellous, Mum', and she stays behind beneath the ancestral portraits, dumbfounded, shattered by mercy.

Even Dürrenmatt's most recent attempt, in 1964, to give his gangster-spectacular a conclusive form, by means of rearrangements, drastic cuts, doing without numerous musical numbers, and the addition of the subtitle 'Opera of a Private Bank' has failed to bring any elucidation to the far too grandly conceived dramatic fresco. The bold connection with Shakespeare's history plays, their heroic world, their dramaturgy, their language, the parodied tone of the tragedies (also of those by the young Schiller and the old Goethe) do indeed create a style, but not a world. 'In the theatre a super-reality must be opposed to reality. Fiction must be preceded by "myths", otherwise they are meaningless.' So much for Dürrenmatt's theory concerning *Frank V*. The fact that the super-reality demanded does not in this, of all plays, take on any tangible shape is not due to any artistic deficiency, but to the lack of an authority which governs all the action, to the lack of a central idea, of an effective inspiration which would hold together the model-world and the drama. This massive torso, in which are contained some of Dürrenmatt's boldest, most provocative variations on the theme of 'mercy and justice' lacks the dramatic mainspring which he himself in his speech on receiving the Schiller-Prize has called 'the poetic fable'. It is from this alone that myths can proceed.

9
The Physicists

The political situation of physics in the middle of this century has been discussed ad nauseam. The idealistic postulate of open and unrestricted research is irreconcilable with the desire for secrecy on the part of those who for reasons of power politics finance research on an immense scale. Physics is – from a social but not a scientific point of view – caught in a dilemma, in what amounts to an insoluble situation. This impasse does not match up to the demands of drama; plays which nevertheless deal with this, 'the most fundamental human problem since the emancipation of women', and which take, for instance, a physicist's struggle with his conscience, and unearth in it a tragic conflict (of almost classical dimensions) between duty and inclination, tend to fail because their dramatic structure absolutely insists that there be a decision, that the problems be solved. And such an outcome, whichever way it is considered, can be conclusive only in a theatrical sense; it can have no effect outside. Even Dürrenmatt's physicists are allowed to settle the battle with their consciences and win through to a heroic self-sacrifice, yet they do so in a situation which immediately reveals to them with utter clarity the ineffectiveness of their attitude. Dürrenmatt has found the type of drama which is appropriate to the intractable *situation* of physics, because it allows him to reveal this intractability in a style which creates the maximum tension, namely the *situation* comedy.

This type of drama, usually called 'farce' and generally looked down upon, despite Wedekind's attempts to ennoble it (as, for instance, in *The Love Potion*), has the following characteristics: (*a*) Unlike pure comedy, it creates tension not by letting the audience in on the tricks which are being played on the hero, but by cunningly misleading the spectators and by means of startling surprises; (*b*) the characters do not assert their true identity at the beginning; almost invariably they wait until an effective climax before throwing off their disguise, and revealing their 'true selves'; (*c*) the setting for a farce is a room with numerous doors which allow rapid, effortless alteration of the numbers of characters on stage and unexpected entries at every suitable or unsuitable moment.

All these structural characteristics are to be found in *The*

Physicists. Yet Dürrenmatt has not labelled his play a farce (it is too serious for that) but with unmistakable irony has indicated that it keeps strictly to the Aristotelian unities of time, place and action: 'The action takes place among madmen and therefore requires a classical framework to keep it in shape.' Indeed, many a fin-de-siècle farce looks like a comical twin brother of the Ibsenesque analytical drama; but the fact that classical tragedy started from a different assumption is carefully explained by Dürrenmatt in his essay 'Problems of the Theatre' (1954). Roughly speaking he says that the severity of form and the concentration of an analytical drama like *Oedipus Rex* were only possible because the audience already knew the story and thus relieved the author of the necessity of loading the beginning of his work with a tedious exposition. Thus the drama, which did not begin until almost everything had already happened, could derive its intrinsic vitality from the unfolding of its background history; surprising for the heroes, not for the audience.

As we have said, in the case of *The Physicists*, it is different. Dürrenmatt insists on cunningly misleading the audience even in the long, novelistic introduction to the published version of the play, where he introduces his three physicists, in-patients in a luxurious mental hospital, as 'harmless, lovable lunatics' who have an unfortunate and incomprehensible tendency to strangle their nurses. In reality – to begin with the background history – it is of course quite a different story. Fifteen years previously the young gifted physicist Johann Wilhelm Möbius published his dissertation on the fundamental principles of a new physics; but then, having considered the possible applications of his theory, he came to an almost suicidal decision:

> I was poor. I had a wife and three children. Fame beckoned from the university; industry tempted me with money. Both courses were too dangerous. I should have had to publish the results of my researches, and the consequences would have been

D

the overthrow of all scientific knowledge and the breakdown of the economic structure of our society. A sense of responsibility compelled me to choose another course. I threw up my academic career, said no to industry and abandoned my family to its fate. I took on the fool's cap and bells. I let it be known that King Solomon kept appearing to me, and before long, I was clapped into a madhouse.

Twelve years passed, lonely and undisturbed. Möbius worked out in his cell the Unitary Theory of Elementary Particles and the Principle of Universal Discovery. Then – by chance, independently of each other – two other physicists came across his dissertation and recognised its fundamental significance; one in the East, the other in the West. Both started investigations, brought in their country's Secret Service which tracked down Möbius, and, feigning schizophrenia, they had themselves interned in the same sanatorium as Möbius, one calling himself 'Einstein', the other 'Newton'. Despite the closeness of their daily contact they apparently failed for many months to see through each other or Möbius. In fact complications arose: they were recognised as sane by their nurses – whom love did *not* make blind but more perceptive. They saw themselves compelled, for reasons of security ('My whole mission hung in the balance, the most secret undertaking of our Secret Service') and as irrefutable evidence of their madness, to murder their nurses; first Newton, and three months later Einstein.

It is at this point that the comedy begins; the exposition of the background history is left over until Act Two. In the meantime, in the brilliantly executed false exposition of Act One, a gruesome humour prevails, arising from the admixture of detective thriller and lunatic asylum. The setting: the drawing room of an isolated wing of the sanatorium whose only occupants are the three physicists, each in his own cell. On the stage: detectives, busy dealing with the corpse, and Head Nurse Marta Boll, 'looking as resolute as she really is',

giving them information. She does not permit Detective
Inspector Voss to smoke or have a glass of brandy nor even
to question the murderer, or rather – since 'the poor man's
ill, you know' – the assailant. The physicist Ernesti is playing
the violin in his cell ('because he thinks he is Einstein he can
only calm down when he's playing the fiddle') and the doctor-
in-charge is accompanying him on the piano, so Voss cannot
talk with her, either. Inspector Richard Voss gives orders
for the corpse to be taken out, sends away his men and
Sister Boll and settles down to wait. Newton appears, dressed
in a costume appropriate to his era ('in reality', as we learn,
a mad physicist by the name of Beutler), lights a cigarette
for himself (but forbids Voss to do the same: 'only the
patients are allowed to smoke here') and enquires about the
cause of the disturbance. Voss explains what has happened.
'How on earth could anyone bring himself to strangle a
nurse?' says the astounded Newton. When Voss reminds
him that he did the same thing three months ago he is
indignant: 'That was something quite different, Inspector.
I'm not mad, you know . . . My mission is to devote myself
to the problems of gravitation, not the physical requirements
of a woman.' Then he confides his secret to Voss; he is only
pretending to be Newton so as not to confuse poor Einstein –
'in reality', he himself is Einstein. Voss (like the audience) is
perplexed. But even more paradoxical revelations follow:

NEWTON. You're cross, aren't you, because you can't arrest me?
INSPECTOR. But Albert –.
NEWTON. Is it because I strangled the nurse that you want to
    arrest me, or because it was I who paved the way for the
    atomic bomb?

Beutler – who thinks he is Einstein but pretends to be
Newton – explains that knowledge gained by physicists is
treated by engineers 'as a pimp treats a whore . . . So any
fool nowadays can switch on a light or touch off the atomic

bomb . . . if you don't understand anything about electricity, why don't you refuse to turn on the light?' Newton departs with the recommendation: 'Richard. You're the one who should be arrested.' In this lighthanded fashion, on this amusing level the theme of the play is given its first airing.

The Doctor-in-charge, Fräulein Doktor Mathilde von Zahnd comes in, an old hunchbacked spinster, 'last notable offspring' of a mighty dynasty of generals and politicians. Now, at last, Voss may smoke, for even she allows herself a cigarette, 'Sister Boll or no Sister Boll.' The Fräulein Doktor has no medical explanation for the murder of the two nurses (she thinks it possible that 'radioactivity affected the brains' of the physicists); in any case, she is ready to fall in with the public prosecutor's request that she replace the nurses (who in fact were also selected for their physical strength – one a wrestler, the other a judo champion) by muscular male attendants. In the middle of this conversation, Einstein appears for a moment, gently, dreamily, his fiddle under his arm. Immediately afterwards the entry of Möbius, the third physicist, is at last announced. His wife has arrived with their three adolescent sons to say farewell; she has married a missionary and is to emigrate to the Mariana Islands in the Pacific.

Then a gawky, deadly serious man, obsessed with visions of King Solomon, steps forward to meet his ex-wife, who greets him: 'my little Johann Wilhem, my dear, dear little Johann Wilhelm.' Then he meets Missionary Oskar Rose, 'a good man through and through' ('a passionate father', he brings six sons with him into the marriage), who ends every sentence with a pious text from the Scriptures. Finally there are his three, well-brought up boys who take out their recorders and play a trio by Buxtehude. The scene is full of haphazard comic effects, a pot-pourri, the comedy of which can only be justified as a contrast to Möbius's elemental outburst of despair which follows it. Squatting inside an upturned table, as if it were a space capsule, he assaults his

family with 'A Song of Solomon to be sung to the Cosmonauts': the lurid vision of a spaceship adrift in outer space
amongst the lead fumes of Mercury and the methane pulp of
Jupiter. Then Möbius chases away his family with ferocious
curses: 'May you sink and rot in the blackest hole of the
sea, forgotten by God and man!'

Nurse Monika calms his fury and brings him back to
reason. 'You were putting it on,' she announces quite frankly,
and Möbius, his disguise penetrated, ashamed of himself,
says in self-justification: 'If you're in a madhouse already the
only way to get rid of the past is to behave like a madman.
Now they can forget me with a clear conscience.' Nurse
Monika carries on, talking quite openly to him: she does not
believe Möbius is mad: in fact, she believes firmly that King
Solomon does appear to him and dictates physical formulae
to him. She admits her love for him – despite the warning:
'It is fatal to believe in King Solomon' – and forces him to
confess: 'I love you too, Monika. More than my life. That is
why you are in danger.' Einstein drifts across the stage:

> Nurse Irene and I were in love too . . . I warned her . . . I
> implored her to run away . . . She wanted to marry me. She
> even obtained permission for the marriage from Fräulein Doktor
> von Zahnd herself. Then I strangled her. Poor Nurse Irene. In
> all the world there's nothing more absurd than a woman's
> frantic desire for self-sacrifice.

He goes, saying: 'And you be sensible too, Nurse. Obey the
man you love and run away from him; or you're lost.' Monika,
her impetuosity strengthened by the power of love, remains
unshakeable; she wants to marry Möbius, go away with him
('Fräulein Doktor von Zahnd has already arranged everything') and help him to spread word of Solomon's revelations
throughout the world. 'I am here to help you, to fight at
your side. Heaven, that sent you King Solomon, sent me
too.' Möbius ('I love you, Monika, good God I love you.

That's what's mad') answers only in monosyllables, then draws her to the window (MONIKA: 'You have tears in your eyes.' – 'So have you.' – 'Tears of happiness') and strangles her with the curtain cord . . . This scene is too boldly conceived and so abrupt that it is almost impossible to act; it demands ecstasy while the dialogue remains spare and dry, in tune with the lapidary language of the whole play, compressed almost to the level of formality.

The beginning of the second Act is a brilliant inversion of the first scene. Once again Inspector Voss and his men are busy with the corpse of a nurse, but this time he is immediately offered brandy and a cigar (which he declines) and this time the Fräulein Doktor refers to 'the murderer' and allows Voss to correct her: 'the assailant' (whom he does not wish to interrogate at all). When his men have finished their work, he orders: 'Take the body out. Again.' Möbius rushes in, bids a silent farewell to the deceased and asks the Inspector to arrest him. Voss refuses: 'You yourself admitted that you acted under the orders of King Solomon. As long as I'm unable to arrest *him* you are a free man.' He becomes almost euphoric:

> At first I felt angry at not being able to proceed with the arrests. But now? All at once I'm enjoying myself. I could shout with joy. I have discovered three murderers whom I can, with an easy conscience, leave unmolested. For the first time justice is on holiday – and it's a terrific feeling.

In other words, the justice which holds sway in Mathilde von Zahnd's empire is peculiar and arbitrary. There is no fear of any further murders, for in the meantime three he-man attendants have taken up their duties, international heavyweight boxers, enviously eyed by Voss: 'If only we had them in the police.' There is nothing else here of interest to ordinary justice, so Voss can go.

The attendants have served dinner and for the first time all three physicists meet on stage, without witnesses – therefore we can expect revelations. At first Newton and Möbius are alone; Newton is upset by the new security measures, but more interested in the menu: liver-dumpling soup, poulet à la broche cordon bleu. Consuming course after course, he betrays his secret at a pace geared to the succession of dishes. He is not Newton, not Einstein, nor even Beutler; 'My real name, dear boy, is Kilton.' And even before he has finished admitting that he is engaged on a Secret Service mission, Einstein is standing there revealing that he is really the Secret Agent Eisler – revolvers are drawn, then they agree on an amicable discussion. The wooing of Möbius begins: 'Come on out: within a year we'll have you in a top hat, white tie and tails, fly you to Stockholm and give you the Nobel Prize,' promises Newton and he justifies his approach by saying:

It seems to me, if it can restore the greatest physicist of all time to the confraternity of the physical sciences, any military machine is a sacred instrument. It's nothing more nor less than a question of the freedom of scientific knowledge. It doesn't matter who guarantees that freedom. I give my services to any system, providing that system leaves me alone. I know there's a lot of talk nowadays about physicists' moral responsibilities. We suddenly find ourselves confronted with our own fears and we have a fit of morality. This is nonsense.

Einstein can call upon a different ideology:

If we are physicists, then we must become power politicians. We must decide in whose favour we shall apply our knowledge, and I for one have made my decision. Whereas you, Kilton, are nothing but a lamentable aesthete. If you feel so strongly about the freedom of knowledge why don't you come over to our side? . . . Our political system too must eat out of the scientist's hand.

Möbius remains silent. Revolvers are drawn again, this time to settle the destination of the manuscripts – but Möbius admits that he burned all his notes immediately after the death of Monika.

EINSTEIN. I shall go mad.
NEWTON. Officially we already are.

In the second round of the ideological duel Möbius comes to the conclusion:

> Each of you is trying to palm off a different theory, yet the reality you offer me is the same in both cases: a prison. So I prefer my madhouse . . . Our knowledge has become a frightening burden. Our researches are perilous, our discoveries are lethal. For us physicists there is nothing left but to surrender to reality. It has not kept up with us. It disintegrates on touching us. We have to take back our knowledge and I have taken it back. There is no other way out, and that goes for you as well . . . Either we stay in this madhouse or the world becomes one. Either we wipe ourselves out of the memory of mankind or mankind wipes itself out.

This brings Einstein and Newton round to his way of thinking and together they raise their glasses and drink to the murdered nurses, whose death only now, by this renunciation, becomes meaningful. They are 'mad, but wise . . . Prisoners, but free . . . Physicists, but innocent.'

The key in which this scene is pitched is strange; in it, philosophical and humanitarian truisms are discussed with a certain solemnity, and, despite the madhouse setting, the culinary trappings and the gun-play, with so much earnest rhetoric, that a naïve spectator might think that here at last was a disclosure of the writer's 'real message', done up in a neat package, and a sceptical spectator, fearing the same thing, might feel duped by its banality. Of course the scene offers only a very schematic and skeletal account of the physicist's classic conflict; of course the conversion of the two hard-boiled Secret Agents to heroic self-sacrifice happens extremely abruptly and its motivation can hardly be said to arise from the characters' predispositions; yet this theatrically accelerated unwinding of the incident is justified by its economy of means, because the play has no interest in establishing the private heroism of the three physicists as some kind of salvation of the world: it seeks to reveal the ineffectiveness of such heroism. The scene itself has no effect with regard to the dramatic structure of the play; what happens in it has not the slightest influence on the course or outcome of the play as a whole. Its purpose is to bring the three physicists, in the most direct and plausible manner possible, to a position of maximum elevation from which to fall, to a position in which they are likely to be most severely disconcerted by the ensuing revelation of the futility of all their arguments and resolutions.

The Doctor-in-Charge appears, has the physicists brought from their cells and solemnly reveals to them her secret; another piece of exposition which until now has been carefully kept hidden:

He has appeared before me also. Solomon, the golden king . . . He had arisen from the dead, he desired to take upon himself again the power that once belonged to him here below, he had unveiled his wisdom, that Möbius might reign on earth, in his name . . . But Möbius betrayed him. He tried to keep secret what could not be kept secret. For what was revealed to him was no secret. Because it could be thought. Everything that can be thought is thought at some time or other . . . He did command me to cast down Möbius, and reign in his place. I hearkened unto his command. I was a doctor and Möbius was my patient. I could do with him whatever I wished. Year in, year out, I fogged his brain and made photocopies of the golden king's proclamations, down to the last page . . . I went cautiously about my work. At first I exploited only two or three discoveries, in order to rake together the necessary capital. Then I founded enormous plants and factories, one after the other. I've created a giant cartel. I shall exploit to the full, gentlemen, the Principle of Universal Discovery.

This grandiose tirade, steeped in the torrid language of mysticism, is bound to cast the three physicists into the depths of despair: 'The world has fallen into the hands of an insane, female psychiatrist' – and all three are at her mercy, because of the murders, which brand them as lunatics in the eyes of the world, and which, it turns out, were likewise planned by the madwoman: 'I could count upon your reactions. You were as predictable as automata. You murdered like professionals.'

In view of what has gone before, this last revelation may come as a surprise. In fact, in terms of the dramatic structure, it completes the chain of causes and effects, but is nothing like so plausible as Claire Zachanassian's admission that she herself had bought up and starved Guellen in order to make the citizens ripe for her revenge. Was it really necessary for this all-powerful doctor to risk the uncertainties of a game played with murder and policemen? Could she not simply have put the defenceless physicists under lock and key? (Or: why did she let the two Secret Agents get at Möbius in the first place?) Is there perhaps a motive which we don't know about? Was there a reason for getting rid of the nurses? (Even the fate of the resolute Sister Boll, who in the first Act definitely appeared to possess a degree of power over the Doctor-in-Charge, remains totally unexplained). The posing of such questions demonstrates that Dürrenmatt's plots move almost inevitably to a point where they invalidate their own premises – yet such sophistry is out of place, for Dürrenmatt certainly does not intend to convince by argument but to conquer by theatrical means. Mathilde von Zahnd's triumph must be absolute:

> My cartel will dictate in each country, each continent; it will ransack the solar system and thrust out beyond the great nebula in Andromeda. It all adds up, and the answer comes out in favour, not of the world, but of an old hunchbacked spinster.

The three physicists are left alone on stage. They speak in turn, 'quite calmly and naturally', stating their roles:

'I am Newton, Sir Isaac Newton . . .'
'I am Einstein, Professor Albert Einstein . . .'
'I am Solomon. I am poor King Solomon. Once I was immeasurably rich, wise and God-fearing . . . But my wisdom destroyed the fear of God, and when I no longer feared God my wisdom destroyed my wealth. Now the cities over which I ruled are dead, the Kingdom that was given unto my keeping is deserted: only a blue shimmering wilderness. And somewhere round a small, yellow, nameless star there circles, pointlessly, everlastingly, the radioactive earth.'

How else is this conclusion to be interpreted if not that the three physicists have now gone mad and that from now on they will be 'harmless, lovable lunatics', as the introduction described them? This is the only way Dürrenmatt could fulfil his unambiguous postulate, formulated for the first time in his commentary on *The Physicists*: 'A plot has been thought out to the end only when it has taken its worst possible turning.' Granted, classical tragedy also takes its worst possible turning after its peripeteia, but there it produces a catharsis. Dürrenmatt's heroes sacrifice themselves in vain, their downfall does not contribute to the reconstruction of a shattered world order. For: 'What concerns everybody can only be resolved by everybody. Every attempt by an individual to resolve for himself what concerns everybody, is doomed to failure.' From none of Dürrenmatt's plays can handy lessons be drawn; there are hardly any attitudes or decisions which we can apply to our own lives, but the contorted, often grotesque and paradoxical world of the plays does allow us an insight into the grotesqueness and the paradoxes of our own world – at least that is true of the comedy that plays with the 'most topical' theme of our age: *The Physicists*. Perhaps that is how it must be. Because it reveals so compellingly the futility and ineffectiveness of every reaction, our reaction too must be ineffective, almost unobjective.

Möbius has failed; the deed which so strikingly recalls the end of Brecht's *Galileo* was in vain. Galileo suffered the humiliation of self-denial and imprisonment in order to be able to carry on his work in secret; he had to hand his manuscripts over to the Curia to prevent their being published, but he made secret copies, so as to ensure that use is made of his discoveries after all. Möbius retreats into self-denial and imprisonment in order to be able to carry on his work in secret; he hides his manuscripts to prevent their being published, but the Doctor-in-Charge makes sceret copies so as to ensure that use is made of his discoveries after all. Galileo, inspired by faith in the future sacrificed himself in order to make possible the progress of physics; Möbius, hostile to the future, sacrifices himself in order to hinder the progress of physics. Dürrenmatt counters Brecht's optimism with the pessimism of his anti-Galileo.

10

Hercules and the Augean Stables

'People are always children,' says Dürrenmatt in a note on *It is Written*. He never ceases to trust in the naivety of his audience and to demand naivety from his directors: 'My plays should be staged as if they were aimed at an unsophisticated audience. I should be treated as a sort of conscious Nestroy; that is the way to get the best from my work. Stick to my inspirations and let the profundity take care of itself.' The ideological puzzle-play, *The Marriage of Mr Mississippi*, was followed by the 'magical comedy' (in the style of Raimund or the early Nestroy), *An Angel Comes to Babylon*; the intellectual parlour-game, *The Physicists*, is followed by *Hercules and the Augean Stables*, puppet theatre with live actors, a children's play for adults, totally naïve in its tranquillity and its humour, a hearty, easy-going satire, no meat for an alert intellectual metropolitan audience but nourishing fare for the provincial repertory audience. The 1954 radio-play had already been adapted for the stage on a number of occasions (principally by school or amateur dramatic societies). The development of the material into a proper play seems to have tempted Dürrenmatt to test the capacity of a modest, quite respectable story to stand up to the immediacy of narration and illustration on stage. This is a further development of the tendency to make comic material out of Wilder's brand of anti-illusionism, thus, for example, 'four cows which exist only in the imagination of the audience' are evoked in rich, almost poetic language, then patted and milked; an appeal to the audience's delight in using its imagination to enter into the spirit of the play.

This entertaining theatricality, which leaps around with space and time at will, now in fact tends to cover up the drama and to conceal the strength of that element which, since *Frank V* and *The Physicists*, has gained increasing significance in Dürrenmatt's theoretical utterances: chance. Contrary to all classical philosophies of the drama, according to which chance (the author's arbitrary power) is prohibited because it counteracts strict causality, Dürrenmatt now explains: 'The playwright's art consists in introducing chance into the action in the most effective way possible . . . The more people act according to plan, the more chance is able to affect them . . . Chance affects them worst when, because of it, they reach the opposite of their goal.' The comedy of

Hercules is the first play to be dominated with a certain consistency by chance; again and again it cheats the hero out of the rewards of his exertions. 'Life is not fiction!' comments Polybius, the hero's private secretary; 'There is no justice, least of all poetic justice; anyone who sets himself a goal reaches the opposite; anyone who asserts his rights is defeated.'

In Dürrenmatt's travesty of mythology a contrary fate transforms all Hercules's heroic labours into failures. We learn about the first three from the dialogue and the play begins with the lamentable conclusion of the fourth: Hercules has successfully hunted the boar of Erymanthus as far as Mount Olympus – but there the beast falls into a ravine, before his very eyes. Even the cleansing of the Augean stables (according to the legend, it was completed in one day, when Hercules diverted the water of two rivers through the stables) is hindered. Hercules is the victim of the hostile workings of chance right up to his death (which is anticipated at the beginning of the play). Deianeira sends him the shirt of Nessus in order to secure his love for ever but achieves the opposite effect – the poisoned garment kills Hercules.

Dürrenmatt has turned the Augean stables of the legend into a country inhabited by primitive peasantry called Elians who are literally choking in dung. Augeas, President of the primitive democracy (which Dürrenmatt stamps with the unmistakable imprint of Switzerland), persuades his fellow-citizens (they have names like Pentheus of Säuliboden, Cadmus of Kasingen, Sisyphus of Milchiwil), who are up to their waists in dung, to hire Hercules as dung-remover. The hero is so deeply in debt that he has to accept this unheroic offer whether he likes it or not. Together with his beloved Deianeira, and Private Secretary, Polybius, whom he is in the habit of throwing downstairs in moments of rage, he enters Elis. Yet Hercules is unable to start the cleaning because the Elians have had second thoughts. What will become of the lucrative export of compost? What of the army, which is specially trained for the war against dung? What of the Elian virtue, which is rooted in the soil, 'if the traditional comfort of the dung is removed'? For the sake of the theatrical effect we must accept the fact that all these arguments, presented in a pithy satire on Parliament, only come to light long after the decision to remove the dung has been taken.

The action stagnates, so Hercules has time for a fatherly chat with Iole, Augeas' adolescent daughter, who has fallen in love with him:

> I am stronger than other men, and therefore, because I need not be afraid of any man, I do not belong to the human race. I am a monster like those saurians which I root out of the marshes. Their time is up, and so is mine. I belong to a bloody world, Iole, and I live by a bloody trade.

And Deianeira, embodiment of Greek culture and humanity, has time to awaken in Phyleus, son of Augeas, a feeling for the beauty of this world and of what mankind has made of it. But Phyleus is afraid of a future without dung: 'Because we do not know how to live without dung. Because nobody will reveal to us the potential of mankind, his capacity to do great and beautiful things, true and brave things.' And Hercules – who in the meantime has been forced by shortage of money to perform feats of weightlifting, and to wrestle with wild beasts in the Elian National Circus – knows, too, that he alone cannot civilise Elis, and urges Deianeira to marry Phyleus:

> I undertake to shift mountains of filth, to do the dirty work that only I can do, but you can bring spiritual fulfilment, beauty and sense to the country, once it has been cleansed. Thus we are both needed by Elis, its only possible hope of becoming human. Stay with Phyleus, Deianeira, and my dirtiest work will be the crown of my career.

But all these beginnings are without success, both idealistically and dramatically. Hercules does not get permission for the feat, 'because the place where the dung is deepest is in the minds of the Elians'. So he leaves and heads for an even dirtier feat of heroism; Polybius and Deianeira, who has left Phyleus standing at the altar, go with him. Iole creeps along behind him (we know from the death-scene that she will be his last mistress, bringing death to him through Deianeira's jealousy). Augeas lets Hercules go ('He is the one and only possibility, which comes, then goes'); then he reveals his secret to his son Phyleus: a garden full of flowers and fruit.

I am a politician, my son, not a hero, and politics doesn't work miracles. It is as weak as people themselves, a symbol of their fragility and destined for constant failure. Politics never does anything good if we ourselves do not do good. So I did good. I transformed dung into compost. Times are hard, and one can do little for the world, but we should at least do what little we can. We should make our own contribution. The Grace by which our world might brighten cannot be forced into being, but you can make the assumption that Grace – if it comes – will find in you a pure mirror for its light. So let this garden be yours. Do not refuse it. Be like it; transformed deformity. Bear fruit yourself. Dare to live, and to live here, in the midst of this shapeless, desolate country, not as one who is contented but as a malcontent who spreads his discontent and in time changes things. The heroic task which I now give you, my son, the labour of Hercules which I now shift onto your shoulders.

The comforting wisdom of this final turn of the plot (the 'best possible', so to speak) now of course invalidates the starting point of the whole play; how can we understand that Augeas himself sent for Hercules although he not only already knew that the hero would not perform the labour but had himself long ago found a much more sensible way of conquering the dung problem? It is therefore not the pious optimism of this ending which is fatal but the inconsistency

of the whole design (which of course has nothing whatsoever
to do with a dramatic theory that endorses 'chance'). It is
not even corrected by the pessimistic ending which Dürrenmatt added after the première: Phyleus refuses the garden
and rushes in pursuit of Hercules in order to try to win
Deianeira's hand after all (Hercules, as we know, will kill
him). The Elians (Why doesn't Augeas urge them to start
cultivating the soil with the aid of the compost?) warn the
audience in a gloomy final chorus that they should do in
their own world what the Elians did not manage to do in
theirs.

This work represents an astonishing failure, for it is by
no means a grandiose, self-complicating design like, say,
Frank V. On the contrary it is a play which fulfils its aims
completely, a play not without humour and a robust kind of
wit – but just overwhelmingly innocuous: the first play by
Dürrenmatt which in no respect tries to expand the limits
of theatrical possibility. It is free of those antitheses and
paradoxes which can rouse and move an audience.

I I

The Meteor

Very slowly – and perhaps in theory earlier than in practice –
Dürrenmatt has developed the idea of a dramaturgy of
events, in which chance has a constitutive function. The
manifestations of lightning and uranium in *Frank V* (which
still stood out like foreign bodies in the organism of the play)
were the first attempts. From them it was discernible that

chance, if it is to be theatrically effective must be highly improbable, in fact totally incredible. Even the traditional
dramatic theory of casuality acknowledges the validity of
minor manifestations of chance, or manages to give them an
appearance of necessity by adding in extra motivations.

Everything that happens on the stage has naturally been
planned intentionally by the author, though his choice of
events is in a sense arbitrary. In classical drama chance is not
admitted because it is detrimental to that inner necessity, to
the cogency of the events which makes an incident seem
'rational' and elevates a man's life into his 'fate'. Dürrenmatt
rejects this stage-causality not because it is mechanical, but,
because its mechanicalness – even in naturalistic plays which
set out to give a realistic picture of life – blindly imputes to
everything a 'sense', which in reality events do not have.
Dürrenmatt's stipulation that life in an indiscriminately
hostile natural environment is at the mercy of the most
irrational chance occurrences, and must therefore be reflected
in similarly constituted plays, is therefore to a certain extent
'naturalistic', in its central idea, though not in its treatment of
illustrative detail.

A good example of this is *The Meteor*, the first Dürrenmatt
play to have a metaphorical or allegorical title: the annihilating impact of a meteor symbolising chance in an irrational,
indiscriminately hostile natural environment. Dürrenmatt's
dramaturgic premise is the most improbable and incredible
of all chances, one which is so improbable and incredible that
we paradoxically impute to it, rather than to any irreproach-
able causality, a metaphysical sense and call it a 'miracle' – the
resurrection from the dead. Dürrenmatt's hero, Wolfgang
Schwitter, when he comes on stage, has died and (to express
it unmetaphysically for safety's sake) has come back to life.
He dies a second time in the interval between the two Acts
of the play and comes back to life a second time. It may be
assumed that this process continues: 'What he achieves is

not eternal life but eternal dying,' says Dürrenmatt in a commentary on the play.

This fantastic or 'metaphysical' premise of the play must be accepted (a discussion of its possibility or probability would be truly grotesque). But the difficulty of making it 'credible', and therefore acceptable as a theatrical event, is not slight. The fact that dead people on stage rise up again does not necessarily prove that a ressurrection has taken place (in fact it happens frequently in *The Marriage of Mr Mississippi*). In order to give this incredible event a semblance of 'reality', Dürrenmatt has to refrain from introducing any other kind of incredibility or any shattering of illusions. He has to build up round this one colossal manifestation of chance a straightforward causal play which follows the conventions of a drawing-room farce à la Wedekind. Yet despite the brilliance which Dürrenmatt brings to bear in making this event 'credible', it remains an assertion which meets an oddly basic resistance from the audience. (Even Friedrich Luft, the critic who praised *The Meteor* most lavishly after its première, did so from an initial assumption that Schwitter was not really dead but only seemed to be so.) The theatre can 'convince' us that a man, who collapses with a rattling noise in his throat and then lies still, is 'dead'. If, however, he gets up again, we think that he simply cannot have been dead. We are more prepared to regard the famous doctor who certified death as a quack than we are to believe in a resurrection. It obviously demands a 'quality' of being dead which is beyond the powers of a comedy – but maybe in reality it would not be any different.

What makes the idea behind *The Meteor* so provocative is precisely this incredibility: it strikes at the core of what we call 'faith'. The incomprehensibility of death is the root of all religions: each in its own way promises, as a way of giving the event a meaning, the conquest of death: resurrection in some shape or form. With all the naivety which the theatre allows, Dürrenmatt enacts a kind of test-case: how would people react as victims or witnesses to the resurrection, which for the faithful Christian must be an undisputable article of his faith, and yet here and now appears to be totally incredible? The victim does not believe in it at all; in fact he protests furiously against it and demands the death to which he has as much right as anyone. The fact that he wants to die and cannot turns him into an anti-Everyman figure: he has been condemned – by blind, senseless chance – to life, and that drives him into a position of radical negation of life.

Dürrenmatt's 'Lazarus' is a world-famous, Nobel Prize-winning dramatist called Wolfgang Schwitter, a vital genius, a literary Prometheus (and possibly also a literary hack):

> When I started writing I had no worries. I had nothing in my mind but my ideas, I was given to boozing and was anti-social. Then came success, prizes, honours, money and luxury. My first wife slept with a tailor to get me a blue suit. The next two only concerned themselves with literature: they organised my fame and my royal household, whilst I was torturing myself to become a classic. The Nobel Prize did the rest for me. A writer whom modern society takes to its heart is corrupted forever.

Such attacks give the play certain characteristics of a satire on literature – again reminiscent of Wedekind (Dürrenmatt's radio-play *Incident at Twilight* may be regarded as a first step). At the same time, within the literary work which deals with death, literature becomes visible as a kind of counter-world in which the fictions cannot stand up to the 'reality' of death. Schwitter's death (or inability to die) leads him to a reckoning with his own life and work:

> Faced with the monstrous disorder of things I locked myself in an imaginary world compounded of reason and logic. I changed places with the products of my imagination because I could not take to real ones, for reality is incomprehensible when one is

sitting at a writing desk . . . My life was not worth living. Then came the pains, the injections, the knife. Realisation came, and knowledge. It was no longer possible to retreat into a world of fantasy. Literature left me in the lurch. There was nothing left but my old, fat, gangrenous body. There was nothing left but horror. So I let myself go. I fell and fell and kept on falling. Everything was now weightless, valueless, senseless. Death is the only thing which is real, which is permanent. I am no longer afraid of it.

The setting for the play is a romantically dilapidated artist's studio on a hot summer's afternoon – the longest day of the year. The young painter Nyffenschwander ('I paint life') is just in the process of painting a nude portrait of his wife, Auguste, when Schwitter comes in: 'Unshaven, wearing an expensive fur coat despite the stifling heat, carrying two suitcases which are so full they could burst at any time. Under his left arm are tucked two massive candles.' He has fled, so he explains, from the hospital. He wants to die, unmolested by doctors and gadgets, in this studio, where he began his career once upon a time as a budding genius. He rents the studio for a while, burns his last manuscripts and climbs into bed to die. The curtains are drawn to, candles are lit. ('Almost like Christmas,' thinks Auguste), then Schwitter asks to be left alone.

Dying's great, Nyffenschwander, you ought to try it sometime! Oh, the thoughts that come to mind, the inhibitions that disappear, the insights that occur to you! Great, just great. But now, don't let me disturb you any longer. Leave me alone for a quarter of an hour, and when you return, I'll be gone.

When Schwitter is alone he gets out of bed again and begins to burn the contents of his suitcases in the stove: it is money, a million and a half, which he does not wish to leave to his heirs. The door opens, a pale clergyman comes in: 'I am Father Emanuel Lutz from the parish church of St. James and I have just come from the hospital.' Schwitter is not to be put off: 'As soon as I've finished burning my fortune, I'm going to lie down and then you'll hear my death rattle.' Father Lutz: 'But Herr Schwitter.' Now for the first time, the catchword 'resurrection' is used – Dürrenmatt makes the audience familiar with this fact by devious means: first as a religious joke:

> FATHER LUTZ. You have risen from the dead. Scientifically that is nothing to get excited about. All hell was let loose at the hospital. The stronghold of unbelief trembled. I am giddy with joy . . . The miracle, the excitement, the immediate proximity of the Almighty . . .
>
> SCHWITTER. Risen from the dead? Me? what a joke!
>
> FATHER LUTZ. God has chosen you, Herr Schwitter, so that the blind will see the light and the godless will believe in Him.
>
> SCHWITTER. Don't start being blasphemous. (*Carries on burning his money.*)
>
> FATHER LUTZ. But, your soul –
>
> SCHWITTER. I haven't got a soul. There was no time for that. Write a play once a year and you say good-bye to things of the spirit . . . Then you disintegrate into your component parts, into water, fat and minerals and you lash out at God and miracles . . . I want to die an honest man, without fiction and literature.

Schwitter who feels by no means miserable at the idea of death – on the contrary, he grows more and more cheerful – begins to hit the brandy bottle hard. By way of contrast Father Lutz, suffering from a chronic heart ailment, sinks weakly on to the bed. His lost faith restored by Schwitter's resurrection, he can now die, peacefully reconciled with God: the first victim of Schwitter's frenzied quest for death. Nyffenschwander, Auguste and the concierge have to remove the priest's corpse in a hurry, for Schwitter is energetically laying claim to the bed for his own death ('I am a Nobel Prizewinner'). 'There you are, Herr Schwitter, the bed's vacant again,' says Auguste. The Nobel Prizewinner once more lies down alone to await death. And once more he is disturbed: 'The Great Muheim stamps in, a lively eighty-year-old interior decorator, building contractor and property owner.' He comes into this studio by chance, almost for no reason at all and he too is destroyed by Schwitter because he interrupts his dying. Schwitter confesses that forty years ago he had an affair with Muheim's wife, and this brings Muheim's world crashing down in ruins for he had built his whole life on his faith in his wife's fidelity: 'Without a happy marriage there are no really gigantic business concerns, without tenderness it's impossible to cheat your way through life, without intimacy you land in the gutter.' Muheim would like to kill Schwitter in despairing rage – 'But dying is sacred to me.'

When Olga enters, Schwitter's fourth wife, a nineteen-year-old ex-call-girl, the embodiment of high-minded trashy sentimentality, Muheim staggers out, a broken man. Because she personally arranged the flowers on Schwitter's death-bed at the hospital, Olga has an unswerving faith in his resurrection: 'Now everything is all right, I shall stay with you.' Yet Schwitter wants nothing more to do with her: 'We said goodbye to each other long ago. Dozens of times. It's gradually getting beyond a joke. Why don't you see sense and get lost!' He had picked her up when he was in a rage, 'angry with myself, angry with the world. I was an old man who wanted to rebel once more'. Now he sends her away, 'back to your trade. You are the gift I bestow on the public. Caesar bequeathed his gardens, I bequeath a whore!'

Schwitter's son, Jochen, appears, a thirty-five-year-old playboy and layabout. He is not interested in his father, only in the inheritance on which he intends to get his hands at the first opportunity. Schwitter shows him the ashes in the stove:

JOCHEN. You don't even hate me. You don't care two hoots about me. So it makes no odds to you if I go to the devil.
SCHWITTER. I'm going to the devil, too, as a matter of fact.

JOCHEN. You are inhuman.
SCHWITTER. Dying *is* inhuman.
JOCHEN. Then get on with it. Die!

Jochen goes ('Besides, I'll still get the royalties'). Olga, who has watched the scene between father and son without saying a word, solemnly takes her leave and follows him. She commits suicide: the second innocent victim of Schwitter's 'resurrection'. Schwitter ('I must say I'm in dazzling form') lies down again, but not to die. Auguste, who has looked after him and plied him with brandy between the various visits, climbs into bed with Schwitter, whilst her husband hammers on the bolted door. This patently farcical conclusion to the Act deliberately reduces into chaos the sequence of scenes, which have been swinging crudely to and fro between philosophy of death and grotesque comedy.

At the beginning of the second Act, an hour later, Schwitter is once more dead, ceremoniously laid out surrounded by wreaths in the studio. His publisher, reporters and inquisitive onlookers are present. The vitriolic critic Friedrich Georgen makes an obituary speech in honour of Schwitter:

> This man who rejected tragedy, suffered a tragic end. It is in this dark light that we have to look at him, for the first time, perhaps, with severe clarity, as the last desperate man of an age which has set about conquering despair. For him there was nothing but naked reality . . . He lacked faith, and therefore faith in mankind. He was a moralist with his roots in nihilism. He was always a rebel, a rebel fighting to survive his stifling environment. His achievement was the expression of an inner hopelessness, not the reflection of reality: it is not, however, reality which is grotesque, but his theatre.

(With an indefatigable delight in self-parody Dürrenmatt has here collected together all the reproaches which his critics have levelled against him.) Koppe, Schwitter's publisher,

congratulates Georgen: 'Your insolence was overwhelming.
As a literary figure the man is finished. One more edition, on
thin paper, and he'll be forgotten.'

Nyffenschwander and Auguste remain alone with the dead
man. Auguste ('I am proud to have been his last mistress')
packs her things and leaves the penniless and talentless
artist. Suddenly Schwitter moves again; his head complete
with chinstrap emerges from the funeral wreaths. 'The bed's
in the wrong place,' he declares, 'so I'll never be able to die.'
Vigorously, with Nyffenschwander's assistance, he begins to
rearrange the furniture in the room, so that everything looks
just as it did forty years ago. This change in the setting
corresponds to the structure of the play: the second Act
appears to be a reversal of the first. Nyffenschwander, the
deceived and wronged husband, curses Schwitter. 'Your
dying was only an excuse! A refined confidence trick! An
insidious piece of play-acting! An infernal trap!' Schwitter
just laughs at him:

> Listen, Nyffenschwander, I wish I had your worries. Here am
> I, dying again and again, spending minute after minute in the
> murderous heat waiting for a dignified departure into infinity,
> despairing because it won't go right, and you come along with
> your irrelevancies! . . . If anybody ought to pray, then it's you.
> Pray to be relieved of your painting . . . All your art is fit for
> is botching things. You've buried yourself in theory because
> you can't *do* anything. Your wife was lifeless in your arms
> because she is lifeless in your pictures. You can't blame her for
> leaving you.

Nyffenschwander furiously grabs a poker and is about to kill
Schwitter when Muheim comes in and intervenes. ('I alone
have the right to kill Schwitter.') A duel ensues; Muheim
hurls the painter downstairs: Nyffenschwander, the third
victim of the resurrection, is dead. And the only reason
Muheim had come was to look at Schwitter's dead body:

'I wanted to stare at your corpse for hours on end. Basking in the presentiment of a higher justice. Feeling sure that a Lord God holds sway up there.'

Schwitter excuses himself, has the curtains closed again and the candles lit. 'I'll climb back in bed and then I'll get on with dying.' Muheim: 'I certainly hope so.' A laconic dialogue helps to while away the time spent waiting for death: 'Well, go on then! – Just be patient – Die, damn you! – I'm trying my best. – I'm waiting. – Really, I feel fine. – Blast!' Schwitter asks for a final cigar. Once again Muheim questions him about the adultery with his wife – now it all turns out to have been a mix-up, a mistake. 'In my agony I confuse everything!' says Schwitter. 'I made up the whole affair; I thought one of my stories was real.' Now Muheim really is a broken man. He has killed the painter for no reason at all, and now even Schwitter seems to think so, too. Then the police arrive, grab the poker out of his hand and take him away to face a murder-charge: the fourth senseless victim.

As the police came in, so too did Schwitter's personal doctor, Prof. Schlatter, visibly upset: 'That's twice I have certified you dead, and you sit there smoking a cigar.' He carries out a thorough medical check-up on Schwitter: 'It's scandalous that I'm still alive!' Schlatter dejectedly confirms: 'Your constitution is unique. Medicine has just suffered its greatest defeat of the century.' The publisher, Koppe, appears, hardly less disconcerted:

KOPPE. Heaven knows, I'm used to the things my authors get up to. But what you are doing, Wolfgang, is quite beyond me. Sheer genius! . . . Do you really die?

SCHWITTER. Quite definitely.

KOPPE. If only somebody could interpret this in terms of Christianity, my firm would be saved.

SCHWITTER. Not a hope.

KOPPE. We'll see. If I were you, I'd begin to suspect something. To you, dying has almost become a spiritual attitude. You go

about dying with an energy that nobody else can match. . . .
Professor, I shudder to look at you. All due respect to your
skill, but this time you seem to have made absolutely fatal
errors.

Koppe goes. Schwitter implores the doctor to bring his
scandalous life to an end with an injection. 'I've lost count
of the times I was near to injecting you with a lethal dose, out
of pure pity,' says Schlatter; but now it is too late for that:

The rational world is convinced of my foolishness and the
spiritual world is convinced of your resurrection. Now that
really is a catastrophe old fellow. Some think I'm crazy, some
think that God despises me: either way, I get blamed . . . Just
my luck to have a Nobel Prizewinner who rises from the dead!
. . . The publicity is terrible.

The doctor tells Schwitter to return to the hospital ('I'll
really examine these resurrections in detail. I bet that you are
still alive after all, that it's a pure neurotic phenomenon . . .
If I don't prove beyond all doubt that you have died twice, I
won't even be able to make a living in the underdeveloped
countries'), but Schwitter angrily throws him out. 'I shall
put an end to my life,' stammers the doctor as he leaves, 'now
your obsession with death has finished me too.'

Frau Nomsen appears in the doorway, a fat 'old woman,
ripe for the graveyard, over-ripe', dressed in black. She
'waddles' forward and sits down breathing heavily. She is the
lavatory attendant in the Bellevue Hotel, she explains, and –
Schwitter's mother-in-law. All she intended was quietly to
lay a few flowers on his death-bed, but now she is bewildered:
'You are a Nobel Prizewinner and I am a lavatory attendant.
We are worlds apart, so we must keep our distance.' Yet
she very rapidly pulls herself together and, with the talkative-
ness of an old woman who 'knows life', she pours out
family stories and gems of wisdom. She talks about her son,

Waldemar, who, although she gave him the benefit of a first-class education, turned out to be a criminal:

> Not that I had anything against criminals. My mother was one and I believe my father was too. But you don't need an education for that sort of thing – healthy common sense will do. You need education to carry off big deals with less risk than you'd ever manage using the ordinary criminal approach ... The boy mustn't harbour any more illusions. He has to learn to be nothing but a rich man, I keep drumming it into him. He has to live on interest and that's that. I know him. If he starts working for a living, he'll get ideas and land himself straight in jail.

Then she talks about her call-girl racket and Olga, to whose marriage with Schwitter she had objected from the start: 'You were enjoying yourself with her, but that's what she was there for. So why get married? ... No, Herr Schwitter, people like us go grey, begging your pardon, but we don't get married.' Olga's fatal mistake, she says, was that

> she allowed herself the luxury of emotions ... Do you, as a writer, permit yourself feelings in your work? Don't you see, feelings are not for having, they're for making. Whenever the customer requires. Feelings don't belong in business unless it's to make money out of them.

Schwitter has allowed this torrent of confessions to flow over him, without saying a word; now, as Frau Nomsen falls silent – she, too, struck down by a heart-attack, which Schwitter however does not notice – he launches into a reply:

> I envy you. You gave yourself to prostitution, I merely gave myself to literature. Certainly I took great pains to remain respectable. I wrote only in order to earn money. I didn't utter a single moral aphorism or practical precept. ... It is with a certain pride, Frau Nomsen, that I may even state, in addition: from the points of view of business and morality I was not

entirely inferior to you . . . Guilt, atonement, justice, freedom, mercy, love – I renounce these lofty reasons and excuses which man needs in order to regulate himself and prey on others. Life is cruel, blind and transitory. It depends on chance.

When Schwitter realises that Frau Nomsen is dead too, he is overcome by despair: 'They all perished in this accursed studio: the priest, the painter, the Great Muheim, Olga, the doctor and the terrible Frau Nomsen, and I am the only one who must go on living.' His son Jochen appears, insultingly intent once more on settling accounts with his father, and close on his heels follow the Salvation Army, who come to pay homage to Schwitter: 'Hail to thee, O risen One! . . . Thou wast visited according to thy faith! Thou art summoned unto eternal life!' Schwitter screams in a rage of despair:

I am summoned to die, only death is eternal. Life is the dirtiest of all dirty tricks played by Nature, an obscene aberration of carbon, an evil growth on the earth's surface, an incurable scab. We are made from dead material and we decay back into dead material.

And as the Salvation Army glorify him in a psalm of resurrection, with guitar and trombone accompaniment, Schwitter cries from the depths of despair: 'When, oh when will I kick the bucket!'

The theatrical effect created by this Lazarus-comedy is enormous, but it misses the point in a curious way. The directness and laconic brilliance of the dialogue either deadens or swamps the inner tension of the individual scenes: the dynamism of the language is more powerful than the dynamism of the events. Never before has Dürrenmatt made such plentiful use of those strained verbs of his which make every occurrence seem larger than life. 'Uttering a death rattle, exploding, smashing, staring, glowering, stamping, waddling, lurching' are all called for in stage directions; for dying alone Schwitter uses the following anti-euphemistic synonyms: to 'evaporate', to 'dance away', to 'peg out', to 'clear off', to 'wither away', to 'buzz off', to 'breathe one's last', to 'rot away'. No theatrical conflict is capable of producing such exaggerated emotional reactions; and strangely, the very fact of the resurrection has scarcely any impact. The sight of the resurrected Schwitter does not throw anybody out of his stride, nobody is struck dumb; once he has uttered a merely slightly surprised 'Oh!' each character gets on unperturbed with the job of making his point.

Thus the resurrection – the actual *meteoric* event, which was supposed to knock off course and liberate or annihilate anyone who collided with it – remains almost inconsequential. By the end one begins to wonder which of the various misfortunes were really produced exclusively by the resurrection. The destruction of Professor Schlatter and the heart-failure of Father Lutz, certainly. However, all the other catastrophes (the deaths of Muheim, Nyffenschwander, Olga and Frau Nomsen) could just as well be induced by the euphoric rage of a dying man. After all, even Schwitter regards himself as one who is dying, not rising from the dead; he regards his dying as a licence for the monumental lack of consideration with which he conducts himself.

In the attempt to reflect a fundamentally unjust, amoral and chaotic world in a play which is so completely premeditated, so 'obvious' because of its duplications, antitheses and symmetries, so clear and explicit that it renders all 'interpretation' superfluous – in this attempt there is patently a contradiction. The play's precision of form deprives the theatrical coincidences of every element of chance (which ought to be a sort of inverted necessity) – instead of the frighteningly incomprehensible impact of the meteor we are offered a virtuoso display of pyrotechnics, calculated to a 't', but a poor substitute for a catastrophe. 'Creations scream out as they disintegrate, the whole thing is an enormous accident': that is how (in Schwitter's words) Dürrenmatt's world looks – not only irrational but totally anti-rational. A play like *The Meteor*, which is perfectly rational, cannot come to terms with it.

12

The Anabaptists

When Dürrenmatt, the embodiment of calmness, does lose his composure the cause is invariably his own earlier plays: not because he has grown more faint-hearted and now he finds his plays undemanding but because the demands they made were plainly not positive enough, not formulated sufficiently clearly to be understood by the audience – which is still rather more timid than he thinks. In retrospect it seems to him that his first attempts were too adventurous and overshot their target. Thus he tries to learn from his theatrical experience (which is always experience of both stage and audience at once) and to correct the lack of moderation so that he will achieve a direct hit.

Compared with the changes which have been made to *Romulus the Great*, *The Marriage of Mr Mississippi* or *Frank V* in the years since their first performance, *The Anabaptists* is not a revised version which sets out to elucidate and improve on *It is Written*, but an entirely new play that is quite radically different from the old one. For Dürrenmatt, after twenty years, his excessively grandiose beginner's effort is just a quarry to be cannibalised, though, surprisingly, it does occasionally produce a finely tooled block which fits perfectly into the quite different, new structure. This is the way Shakespeare may have made use of existing plays, or how the 'English Comedians' who toured Germany in the late sixteenth and early seventeeth centuries made use of Shakespeare.

It is Written was the very first, by no means careless, but totally instinctive sketch of Dürrenmatt's world: the work of a writer who had hardly any idea of what was and was not effective on stage, who brushed aside all empiricism with the disarming grandeur of a usurper and required of the theatre that it achieve – at whatever price necessary – what he demanded of it. It was a historical revue, held together externally by the events in the story (the chronicle of the Anabaptist Kingdom at Münster), and internally by a series of antithetical figurations; by the conflict between the rich man and the poor Lazarus; between secular obsession with the pleasures of this world and religious obsession with the pleasures of life after death; between the first and the last.

What was obviously lacking in the play, which constantly varies these tensions by changing the people involved, was a central idea; an illuminating inspiration which would not only tie together the themes which are straining to come apart but which also would – thematically and structurally – give them a common perspective. After twenty years, Dürrenmatt has injected just such an illuminating notion into his early play – its effects and consequences have transformed *It is Written* into *The Anabaptists*. Apparently, though, this is not a structural notion but a general idea, in fact the very idea which represents the culmination of Dürrenmatt's thoughts about the drama – on the one hand his theoretical attempt to correlate the world and the theatre by presenting conclusions about the world which he has derived from the theatre as conclusions about the theatre derived from the world, on the other hand his practical attempts to represent the world on that stage. All of this presupposes a definite conception of the world and not merely of the theatre. The idea is to *equate* the world with the theatre and to assume that they are governed by the same laws.

The Anabaptists puts this idea to the test: the hero Bockelson is an obsessed actor who – because no theatre will give him the chance to fulfil himself – makes the world into his theatre; his powerful antagonists are theatre-lovers who are able to appreciate the empire he builds and the catastrophe into which he leads it, as a grandiose theatrical spectacle: 'Great, I think that's great. The fellow is a real actor, theatrical to his toe-nails. The way he dashes off a performance is truly astonishing.' It is not the action of the earlier play which has changed but rather the lighting under which it unfolds. As in *It is Written*, Dürrenmatt uses theatrical tableaux to tell the story of Johann Bockelson from Leyden who rose to be king of the Anabaptists in Münster; the story of Bernhard Knipperdollinck, who gives away all his possessions and lives in abject poverty in accordance with the example of Lazarus, an open sore on everybody's flesh; the story of the ecstatically faithful leader of the Baptists, Jan Matthisson, who – convinced that God will not leave him in the lurch – throws himself single-handed against the Catholic army and suffers a pitifully inconsequential martyrdom; the story of the ninety-nine-year-old, crippled Bishop of Münster who takes up arms against the Baptist Kingdom only sceptically, with resigned cynicism; the story of Knipperdollinck's noble-spirited daughter Judith who sets out – as the biblical Judith set out to kill Holofernes – to kill the Bishop and in so doing is herself killed. Dürrenmatt has transferred almost unaltered many of the characters and situations from the earlier play: but their language and their significance have changed with the principal character.

Only a few 'quotations' remain from the original uninhibitedly lofty language, the hymn-like quality of which spills over into self-parody. *The Anabaptists* is to a large extent dominated by its dry, concise, lapidary dialogue, which

E

is calculated solely for its immediate effect, already familiar from *The Physicists* and *The Meteor*. This dialogue only rarely rises to the level of rhythmic speech or crude doggerel. The ironic historical revue has been firmly fashioned as a history play; all those anachronisms and addresses to the audience, which in the early version destroyed the theatrical reality, have been expunged: on a stage which is equated with the world they have no justification, and allusions to contemporary history take their place. Dürrenmatt has made an excellent job of tying up the loose ends, and by adding several new minor characters he has elucidated the external course of the action. From a purely 'literary' point of view, the matter-of-fact way in which he sacrifices the most profound utterances, the most brilliant lyricism to a comparatively trivial but striking repartee, in order to make his play smoother, wittier, more spirited and more effective, may appear to be an intellectual levelling down. But the new 'inspiration', the new main character is designed to make up for this deficiency.

Johann Bockelson is no longer an ecstatic prophet of the here-and-now, of total worldly indulgence. His passionate avowal of earth against heaven ('I am your son, old Earth. You are my mother and in the night I hear you call. I hear your blood rushing in ancient ravines, holy Mother. I kiss you!') is no longer spoken; it is now out of place. The new Bockelson is egoistic, a cynically hedonistic, unscrupulously opportunistic actor who was once refused an engagement by the Bishop of Münster. His establishment of the Baptist Kingdom now appears almost as an act of revenge by a small-time strolling-player gone wild. Bockelson 'believes' in nothing, he merely 'acts' everything – he is vain, selfish, smug and lusting for applause.

I became a Baptist because of professional wretchedness. / Unemployed, I taught muddle-headed bakers, cobblers, tailors / Rhetoric, and watched them as they stirred up the world / With religious ideas, as if it were mud. / Finally I let them unchain

the dogs of war. / Yes, I even became their King because of a
stray idea. / Now, damn it, they believe in me, / Overburdened
with titles, grotesque honours, offices, ideals. / And the indignant princes, frightened / Because their fixed order is totter-
ing, / Cannot distinguish between the real me and the roles I
am playing / And think I am a raging Heracles, a blood-thirsty
Nero, a dark Tamerlane.

Bockelson is not interested in anabaptism, not inwardly
'committed', but is like an actor who hopes that a particular
engagement will yield a major role, a great triumph. If fate
had given him another chance, he would have used it by
going to the same extremes of unscrupulousness in search of
success. ('A half-hearted play is a bad one: so we must be
prepared to risk our all for our play.') Bockelson's changed
character robs the drama as drama of its inner necessity. He
could easily have produced another play instead of the
Anabaptist Kingdom (that is, instead of Dürrenmatt's *It is
Written*).

Now therefore, blind, senseless fate is everything: nothing
else can make history – according to the equation between
world and theatre, postulated by Dürrenmatt and realised by
Bockelson. When, at the climax of the struggle, Bockelson
urges on his faithful followers, he speaks not as a prophet of
war but as a theatre director:

> Our production is in direct conflict with theirs. For, as we
> support the Holy Spirit with our skill in production . . . so the
> Emperor, the Princes and the Bishop support the Powers of
> Darkness, Reaction and Slavery with their often grandiose
> theatrical inspirations. The danger is great, yet we must per-
> severe, brothers, like actors when the whistling starts and the
> rotten eggs rain down.

Everything is seen in theatrical terms – in this play the
Emperor Charles V could not possibly say (as in *It is Written*):
'It is not we who bridle history: it is history which drags

us through the ages.' Dürrenmatt's world has become ahistorical and has no purpose beyond its own boundaries, and no metaphysics: it is 'Nature', a carousel of catastrophes and comedies, of ideas of salvation and world empires, which flourish and wither like flowers in a meadow. The difference between the kingdom of Bockelson and that of Charles V appears slight even to the Emperor: 'This lousy actor's tiny kingdom, however much we may deride it, is nevertheless an image of our own power, and our empire certainly does not appear to be any less fragile'.

As we have said, Bockelson's antagonists are theatre-lovers: they can appreciate his qualities, but they demand a clear-cut division of the spheres, one which excludes all risk: 'The mischief he is causing now is far greater than the mischief he would have been able to cause on the stage,' says the Bishop of Münster ruefully – the Bishop who refused to employ Bockelson in his court theatre and thereby drove him into 'politics'. Bockelson's antagonists (the Bishop, the Cardinal, the Prince and the Duke of Hesse) foregather on two occasions. First, in the middle of the play, at the court of Charles V, in order to discuss the Bishop's proposal that they mount a campaign against the Anabaptists – but they quarrel with greater passion about their Court Theatre companies:

BISHOP. I disbanded my company, Eminence.
CARDINAL. The only time you disband your company is when you want to form a better one! Have you spoken to my leading character-actor or not?
DUKE. And my leading lady? Has she turned up in your troupe? Yes or No?
BISHOP. She is not classy enough for my liking.
DUKE. Not classy enough! Charles, he thinks she isn't classy enough!
PRINCE. These provincials have no taste!
DUKE. You'll pay for that, Prince. I have taken Eisenach.

PRINCE. In that case I'll attack Giessen.
CARDINAL. Peace.
EMPEROR. I thought it was a question of a complex German inter-state rivalry; in fact it's about leading ladies.
PRINCE. More beer!

And so on. At the end of the play they get together once again, this time before the gates of the shattered city of Münster, and Bockelson, the absolute actor, meets them: disappointed, he turns his back on 'Münster's small-town stock company, forsaken by God and by every patron of the arts . . . You no longer satisfy me / You Germanic hole. / I need applause, an enthusiastic audience'. The great personages of the world generously supply him with this acclaim.

BOCKELSON: You Princes, gathered before the city / Which has defied you for years, / I come before you now. / I played the part of a king / And I delivered mock speeches in truly comic fashion / Riddled with quotations from the Bible and dreams of a better world / Which matched the dreams of the people. / Then, for your amusement, I did what you also do. / I governed, exercised arbitrary power and justice . . . / I was imprisoned – also like you – in the deadly boredom of all power / Which I hand back to you – an act which you cannot accomplish. / The play is over, you Princes without equal. / I merely wore your mask, I was not your equal . . . / Yet I, who created the play for you, the bold thinker, / I expect a laurel wreath and not the hangman!

The Princes are delighted: 'Bravo, what an act! What an artist!' The Cardinal engages him at three times the highest salary in his theatre and has him borne away in triumph in his own sedan-chair.

In interviews Dürrenmatt has occasionally thrown out the amusing rhetorical question about what course world history would have taken if Hitler had not been failed in the entrance examination for the Vienna Academy of Art. In this sense

Bockelson too is a 'failed' artist who throws himself into politics. In the preface to *It is Written* Dürrenmatt considers whether 'current events' are reflected in the play, and recommends that we should 'carefully draw the more fortuitous parallels'. In *The Anabaptists* he vigorously obliterates these still highly coincidental external parallels: Bockelson enacts a distinct 'seizure of power'; a child is publicly praised because it has denounced an enemy of the regime; later – coinciding with the point of time in history when the question 'Do you want total war?' was asked – the people ponder over their fate: 'We just liked to listen to you . . . We just stumbled into it . . . Now we believe in the final victory.' Joachim Kaiser has rendered this happy 'final victory', which the actor Bockelson in fact achieves, in the witty formula – which extends the historical parallel – 'The Honorary Doctor Hitler, who after 1945 gets the well-earned chance to build Brasilia.'

As a minor episode, in miniature format, Dürrenmatt reflects once again that moment when a whim of fate decided Hitler's future and therefore the history of Europe: Emperor Charles V has personally to nominate the members to the Imperial Academy of Painting in Vienna: he rejects a certain, seemingly 'untalented dilettante' called Hagelmeier. However, after the conversation with the Cardinal, the Bishop, the Duke and the Prince about Bockelson, he reverses this decision and accepts Hagelmeier, for 'as a member of the Imperial Academy he can harm nothing but art'. It is so easy for a powerful man to prevent a recurrence of Bockelson or Hitler.

Apart from this Nazi parallel, Dürrenmatt has given this play – which was originally concerned only with the religious questions – another political overtone: The antagonists of the Anabaptists, ecclesiastical as much as secular, are capitalists to whom the irritant is not the heretic element but the communist element in Münster. In *It is Written* the Generals

besieging Münster represented the contemptibly materialistic principle: 'It doesn't matter whom we serve so long as
we get paid.' In the new version this conversation has been
much extended: 'I was always on the wrong side. When they
let you plunder Rome, I defended the bankrupt Pope Cle-
ment.' 'Popes are never any good.' 'The Holy Father forgave
my sins, that's all.' 'Mean, damned mean.' 'Blame God . . .'

Both Generals discuss new business opportunities, art
dealing, for example: ('Modern painting won't last: nobody
takes my Michelangelo'). In addition they are joined by a
commercially successful Mother Courage, with whom in this
version they discuss in much more detail how they must
'lovingly fatten up' the war, so that it will 'show a profit'. The
news that the Baptists have introduced 'common ownership
of property' – i.e., communism – robs the warriors, eager for
booty, of 'all moral inclination'. The highly melodramatic
cursing of the city, with which the General in *It is Written*
urged his troops to attack, is replaced in *The Anabaptists* by a
string of political catch-phrases: 'City of equality! City of
popular unity! City of *humanity*!' (The General thinks this
last is 'a pithy French swear-word').

The masters of the world at the court of Charles V do
not think any differently. They are capitalists. Instead of
that meditation on loneliness (see page 30) Charles V now
says:

> I am from the Aargau. / My ancestors left the little dingy
> Habsburg fortress / Near Brugg in Switzerland / In order to
> create a world-wide concern: with family politics. / An
> undertaking which requires discipline, harshness, unhappy
> marriages and piety, / Particularly piety, for people only like to
> die for religious dynasties. / This is the only way they can get
> the feeling that they are not suffering for any old tribe, / But
> for God, for his Church, and for the unity of the West. / That,
> I believe, is their right – something that nations really should
> be allowed to demand.

His interests, like those of the churches and Princes, are purely materialistic. The Cardinal (a new character whom Dürrenmatt has brought into the play so that he does not have to represent the elderly Bishop, as in *It is Written*, solely as a cynical clergyman, for the sake of a theatrical contrast) cheerfully defends the concept of adult baptism ('My God, a traditional Christian idea; the Germans really are a pious nation') and delightedly applauds their polygamy ('Great, I think it's great . . . We cannot possibly get enraged when we have to chuckle'). The church and the Emperor are indifferent to the problem of anabaptism. Yet they all change their tune abruptly when they learn of the introduction of 'common ownership of property' in Münster. That is a political problem, a revolutionary idea which has a bearing on the here-and-now, and which calls into question their positions of power. So they immediately place their forces at the disposal of the Bishop, not for the purpose of a counter-reformation but for an anti-communist campaign.

These political parallels have little to do with the central equation of the world and the theatre: they are peripheral and change nothing. More interesting is the way the tensions between the main characters are shifted because of the changed function of Bockelson. The unbelieving actor Bockelson can no longer appear as the ideal antagonist of the pious Knipperdollinck. In fact Dürrenmatt has pruned this character drastically, depriving him of his most excessive moments of lyrical self-exaggeration, but not altering him basically, before transposing him into the new play. Yet Knipperdollinck, the rich man who helped poor Lazarus Bockelson to power, the ascetic who dreams of life after death, whose collision with the worldly hedonist formed the core of the earlier play, has lost his antagonist, for this Bockelson no longer exists.

Thus Knipperdollinck, forced out to the fringes of the plot, wanders peacefully through this world in search of God, sadly isolated, literally a character from another play, since he has nothing whatsoever to do with Bockelson's one-man show and also nothing to do with the activities of his adversaries. And sadly isolated he suffers his martyrdom in the end, declaiming to himself – following Bockelson's triumphant exit – the last lines of the old play. This time, however, the tone is more despairing; no longer is he so certain of God's immanence and grace. In *It is Written* he confessed: 'The depth of my despair is merely an image of Thy justice!' In *The Anabaptists* he pleads with God: 'Thou hast scorned none of my gifts / Receive now my despair / The agony which tears me to pieces / The cry from my lips which expires in Thy praise / Lord! Lord!'

At the same point in *It is Written* it was not 'expires' but 'fades away' – far more humble and full of devotion. Is Knipperdollinck really still sure that he will be granted God's grace? 'God is silent,' he has to admit when, in the only completely new scene in the play, which replaces the pompous images of Bockelson's splendour and self-indulgence, he asks God for a sign of grace.

KNIPPERDOLLINCK. Hurl down Thy bolts of thunder, Almighty God. Smash me because of my sins.
BOCKELSON. Great. You really make it sound despairing. Well done.
KNIPPERDOLLINCK. God is silent. (*Stares upwards.*)
BOCKELSON. What is He supposed to answer?
KNIPPERDOLLINCK. Nothing but an empty stage.
BOCKELSON. There is nothing else.
KNIPPERDOLLINCK. I am lost.

In this scene – which takes place on the empty stage of the Bishop's theatre – the equation of the world and the theatre reaches its climax:

BOCKELSON.   On Judgment Day, King Bockelson
                     Appeared before the throne of God.

KNIPPERDOLLINCK. Stark naked and smeared with blood,
He made a speech before the Lord.

BOCKELSON. Angels and cherubim, pale and scared,
Fluttered their mighty wings.

KNIPPERDOLLINCK. Impressed by the horror of the world-theatre
The Heavenly Father resigned.

BOCKELSON. Angels and Saints rushed away.

KNIPPERDOLLINCK. So on God's throne
Sat Baptist King Bockelson.

BOCKELSON. Enjoyed for a heavenly moment,
The author-directed downfall of the world.

KNIPPERDOLLINCK. And to the roar of thunderous applause,
World-history made its final exit.

The fact that in this 'duet' Knipperdollinck is once again
Bockelson's partner is due to more external reasons of
dramatic structure: Bockelson's spiritual adversary is now the
ageing Bishop, although they never exchange a word. He has
lost some of his trust in God, some of the benevolent worldly
wisdom which he radiated in *It is Written*; in his passion
(only now attributed to him) for 'worthless comedies' he
admits there is a trace of escapism:

> The farce of our life / The irksome stumbling flight away from
> truth and in search of it / Becomes, on stage, quite simple, a
> romp, merriment, a pleasurable thrill. / We are all actors in
> reality, enmeshed in guilt, accessories in crime. / We need the
> delusion of free and easy hours, to be mere spectators.

Because of the story in which he gets involved, he gradually
loses the certainty that whilst he 'did not want to change the
world', he led a good life: 'I wanted to stay sane amidst the
madness / I must henceforth go round patching up a rotten
order / A fool! What could be more rational?' An enlightened monk (a newly invented minor adversary) declares
bombastically: 'My reason will subdue this unreasonable
world!' Again, this time humorously: 'In the campaign

against Münster's madness even intellectuals must rush to the front-line!' And to cap it all he suffers a pitifully grotesque shipwreck.

The Bishop, conscious of his helplessness, sinks into defeatism ('For eighty years I have cried to God. Now I am dumb') and finally into despair. He speaks the last words; he suffers the last of the three 'worst possible turnings' – after Bockelson's triumph and Knipperdollinck's martyrdom. Standing, as it were, on the corpse of his victim, Bockelson receives the laurels of praise; Knipperdollinck expires on the rack; the Bishop curses the Creation:

> The blessed broken on the rack, the corrupter blessed / The corrupted are slaughtered, the victors scorned by their victory / The court sullied by the judge. / The knot of guilt and error, of reason and wild rage / Dissolves into infamy. / Grace, Knipperdollinck, stretched out between bloody spokes, denounces me. / Get out of your wheelchair, Bishop of Münster! (*Rises.*) / Stand, ancient one, on your own legs! / Trample underfoot the tattered Bishop's robe, the Cross which is derided by your weakness. / This inhuman world must become more human. / But how? But how?

This is not a rhetorical question (like the one which ends Brecht's *The Good Person of Szechwan*) – this inhuman world cannot help being inhuman: it's inhumanity, it seems, lies in its 'Nature'.

The consistency with which Dürrenmatt balances his equation of world and theatre also means that the same laws are applicable in both. In the theatre, which really, of course, presents a summary, their effects are more easily recognisable. One of the laws is obviously 'Chance', which frustrates every attempt to reach a goal (perhaps every attempt to change the world). From this stems the individual quality of Dürrenmatt's big scenes in all the plays after *The Visit*, which was constructed along consistently causal lines. These scenes have no effect on the progress of the plot, they are

devoid of necessity, they contradict causality. Thus, from a
layman's point of view, one could leave out the central scene
of *Frank V* (in which Böckmann is killed); one could even
omit the great discussion amongst the three *Physicists* on
guilt and responsibility; in *The Meteor* one could pick almost
any of the antagonists and cut him out of the play; and so
on . . . In the middle section of *The Anabaptists* one could do
away with almost every scene, or replace them by a single
action running in a totally different direction.

This method of dramatic construction from case to case
or from effect to effect, which could in principle successfully
destroy traditional theatrical causality, requires a counter-law:
in the theatre, so-called 'chance' is produced by the all-
powerful author himself, intentionally and arbitrarily. The
conditions to which chance is subjected in Dürrenmatt's
world could be formulated as a 'Law of Maximum Theatrical
Effect'. This law determines whether a person in a given
situation has his head cut off – or crowned; whether he wins or
loses a battle, whether he betrays his brother or dies for him,
whether he curses God in his misery or thanks Him for it.
All this is ordained by our 'Law of Maximum Theatrical
Effect' under which Nature, History, Psychology and Morality collapse. It is complete empiricism on the part of the
playwright: an attitude which does not produce a theatrical
effect has no value; no villainy is of any use whatsoever if the
audience is bored by it; high-mindedness is only worthwhile
if it inspires a great scene; the 'worst possible turning' is
always the last possible *coup de théâtre*.

Amid these weirdly illuminating postulates of an autono-
mous theatricality which is valid equally for the world and for
the stage, one can no longer imagine a 'lost world order' as an
object of hope, as a metaphysical vanishing point. Heroes of
self-conquest like Romulus, Übelohe, Akki and Ill ('the lost
world-order is restored within them') will never return to
Dürrenmatt's stage. He has accepted this inhuman world as

'Nature'. Even the despair in which Möbius, Schwitter and the Bishop end up (in accordance with the 'Law of Maximum Theatrical Effect') is ineffective – a mere effect which is incapable of influencing the world.

13
King John

Two queens who disparage each other as 'sluts', 'high-class whores' or 'nymphomaniac grannies'; a knight with a spanner forever cursing and trying to do a plumbing job on his rusty armour; a cardinal sitting trembling in bed, and a king creeping in under the bedclothes to join him: such farcical embellishments (in their way a long-established trade-mark of the well-proven Dürrenmatt sense of humour) ensure that *King John* – an evil, bloody, venomously wicked tale of violence, power and powerlessness and of the idiotic, eternally unquenchable desire for a better world – nonetheless never breaks the bounds of what is acceptable as entertaining, consumer-orientated theatre. Powerful but also occasionally guilty of straining insensitively after mere effects, this play is typical Dürrenmatt. In its sententious directness it is even dangerously *over*-typical Dürrenmatt, and, as such, in its development of character groupings and plot, it offers few surprises, nor does it reveal much in the way of new theatrical horizons. Not so much experimenting with 'Shakespeare' as playing safe.

Shakespeare's *King John*, itself hardly ever performed, is a weak play, which towards the end succeeds in confusing itself in the maze of its own intrigues, a flawed work from Shakespeare's apprentice years, a rewritten version of an older, anonymous play, *The Troublesome Reign*. And yet the play has brilliant moments with dense passages of an almost frenetic verbal fantasy in which the horror of war is captured in bloody images.

The action concerns John of the House of Plantagenet, who, as Richard the Lionheart's younger brother, succeeded, him as King, although John's nephew, Arthur, as son of the eldest brother, may have had more right to the throne. Arthur (Shakespeare made him a little boy whose claims are fought for by a rabid mamma) finds help from Philip, King of France. The English and the French fight an inconclusive battle at Angers, then the kings make peace, horse-trading at the expense, of course, of little Arthur: an English niece of the king is to marry the French Dauphin. In order to finance the war, however, John has ill-advisedly fleeced the churches and monasteries, for which he and his allies are now threatened – slap in the middle of the wedding which is to seal their reconciliation – with ex-communication from the Pope. In order to evade the edict, Philip swiftly breaks off his fraternization with John. Once more the battle-cry rings out, once more it is bloody and indecisive. John retreats back to England with his most precious booty – the little Arthur; the French, urged on by the Pope, give chase.

So far, so good. The calamity in the second half (calamity in the sense of classic play-construction) is first that the precious Arthur, the centre of the action, jumps from his prison tower – a fatal hitch – and then that just when everything might turn out right (John having reconciled himself with Rome and the Pope having called off the French) John gets himself pointlessly and motivelessly poisoned by an obscurantist. His son Henry inherits the crown without opposition.

Even with these hitches something could be salvaged. Much more fatal is that Shakespeare himself is never really interested in this luckless, lack-lustre daredevil John. He is not a villain on the scale of Richard III, yet, considering his doubtful legitimacy, he can hardly be good. The result is an amorphous character, sometimes cunning, sometimes cowardly to the point of cruelty, sometimes nonsensically stubborn, a flabby character, he lacks theatrical 'size'. This means that on the stage he is overshadowed by his most faithful follower, Philip, bastard son of Richard the Lionheart, a prize example of the sort of patriotic bulldog exemplified later by Percy Hotspur – yet cleverer than him: Philip is given the heroic lines that end the play.

What can have tempted Dürrenmatt to become so deeply involved with this play? He says he would not have ventured upon a larger play, one that was playable in its original form; and in the disparate pairing of John and the Bastard he apparently found a constellation which increasingly attracted him and led him increasingly further from Shakespeare. He has manhandled the history of King John in the same way as he wrought *The Anabaptists* out of his own early play, *It is Written*. To be consistent, the resultant Dürrenmatt play ought not to be called *King John* but *The Bastard*.

The little, helpless world-reformer, who stumbled around the hybrid scenery of *The Anabaptists* preaching reason and falling flat on his face, has grown into the sturdy, broad-shouldered Dürrenmatt hero who, still preaching reason, now tries to set to rights a bloody Shakespearian world which has fallen out of joint. Philip the Bastard, who in Shakespeare is a rabble-rousing bully-boy, a red-hot war-monger (he suggests, for instance, when England and France have made their peace at Angers, that both armies should join together in ravaging Angers, so that they should get some fun after all), this bastard embodies and represents in Dürrenmatt the principle of political common sense (an unthinkable principle for Shakespearian heroes, to whom honour and glory are all). Thinking chiefly of the ordinary people, the eternal cannon-fodder, he argues indefatigably that war is an unreasonable (that is, risky and unprofitable) means to political ends and that power is what matters. Often John follows his advice, but sometimes not; nevertheless at the end it seems as if it is the Bastard and his common sense that are guilty of all the catastrophes – if this really were so (but for that the play would have to free itself more decisively from Shakespeare's chain of intrigue), Dürrenmatt's *King John* would perhaps be a compelling parable about the impossibility of changing an evil world without abandoning goodwill and resorting to force.

It is intriguing to compare Dürrenmatt's text with Shakespeare's and to see how confidently Dürrenmatt gathers things up, clarifies them, creates motivations, sharpens contrasts, establishes symmetries, follows through the antitheses of speech and counter-speech, and how in this way small alterations work like a chain reaction in their effect on the larger structure; and so a piece of refined dramaturgical doctoring becomes something quite different, quite individual and quite unlike Shakespeare.

Much of the time Dürrenmatt follows the text of the Schlegel translation with only a few retouches (retouches, though, which constantly emphasise the commercial aspect of politics: where Shakespeare speaks of a war as 'terrible and bloody', Dürrenmatt, altering only one word will call it 'terrible and *costly*'). The crucial alteration is that Dürrenmatt consistently attributes to the Bastard every suggestion that a conflict can be resolved without bloodshed, whereas in Shakespeare it's now Philip of France, now a citizen of Angers, now even John who has such ideas. And so the Bastard becomes the chief animator of the action. He persuades both kings not to destroy themselves militarily but to limit their spheres of interest like 'reasonable' heads of monopoly concerns intent on expediency and profitability.

Unfortunately the Bastard has to remain silent at the intervention of a third monopolist, whose business John has wrecked – namely, the Pope, represented here by a certain Cardinal Pandulph, whose cynically Machiavellian arguments aimed at inciting the kings against each other show him to be a worthy opponent to the Bastard and his more humane sense of logic. But, against all reason, the Bastard has to keep quiet when John challenges the papal edict so that the play can still run along the lines of Shakespeare's plot. This is why Dürrenmatt's skilfully rationalised modification of Shakespeare's King John undergoes his penance; for according to the Bastard's own lights it is hardly likely that he would wait until *after* a deal of unnecessary carnage had taken place before suggesting to the king the idea of atonement through a diplomatic manœuvre with France and the Pope. The antithesis between reason and unreason has broken down. For the final round a new conflict has to be brought into play: imperialism versus socialism.

Shakespeare's confused finale, the murder of John, is provided with a brilliant new motive: John has to undergo a sudden inner transformation and refine himself from a monopoly capitalist into a social reformer who wants to cede his power to the people (and here Dürrenmatt brings in the only incident – suppressed by Shakespeare – which has won the luckless John a place in the school-books: the declaration of Magna Carta). Of course the other monopolists cannot tolerate such socialist plans, so John is speedily done away with on the orders of Cardinal Pandulph. The Bastard, frustrated in his attempt to change the status quo from within, seeks refuge like a Karl Moor, or a Che Guevara, amongst the common people, so as to make long term preparations for the revolution – very long term since he plans to bring an army of Bastards into the world . . .

14

Play Strindberg

Everyone knows, or thinks they know, what *The Dance of Death* is about: the classic case of marriage as hell, the battle of the sexes, primeval hatred, self-destructive passion, etc.; finally also, as Strindberg has written, 'the manifestation of great resignation, without which life is impossible'. This may be so when one reads the play with the eyes of the epoch: Böcklin's painting *The Isle of the Dead* as metaphysical background, overhead a streak of light from the dawning age of Freud, an ubiquitous atmosphere which Dürrenmatt summed up as 'plush multiplied by infinity'.

If one reads the play with the eyes of today, and with today's theatre experiences in mind, then it is impossible to overlook the Ionesco-like absurdity of the free-wheeling dialogue, or the Beckettian 'endgame' situation, or the Dürrenmatt-like grotesqueries of drawing-room rituals. It is not surprising that such a play should tempt a theatre man to want to bring to light, if need be violently, the radical core beneath the art nouveau arabesques. And since it is Dürrenmatt who has taken on this task, it is also not surprising that he unearths a Dürrenmatt play from Strindberg's prototype, a new variation of that 'fearful marriage' which Mr Mississippi, Frank V and other of his characters had already endured.

'August Strindberg's *Dance of Death*, adapted by Friedrich Dürrenmatt' – this official designation obscures the facts of the case: Dürrenmatt has rewritten the play. Strindberg's wide-ranging dialogue, often laden with the pathos of the confessional, has been rigorously reduced to spare, hard-hitting, cut-and-thrust exchanges; all the sorrow and self-pity has been expunged from the characters, so that they now fight their eternal marital duels with ice-cold calculation rather than with Strindbergian fervour; whatever plot there is in Strindberg has been distorted by the addition of different motivation into something grotesque ... In other words, Dürrenmatt has turned the play on its head and, with carefully calculated brilliance, has achieved what he wanted: to take a bourgeois marital tragedy and make of it a comedy *about* bourgeois marital tragedy.

Play Strindberg is the new title of this black joke and the suggestion in it of games-playing is important. The whole battle is presented as a game, as a purely theatrical projection of a battle. Whatever the characters take into the field in the way of ideas, admissions, reproaches is only worth something if it can be used as a weapon at that particular moment at that particular stage in the contest. The whole complex of memories, anxieties and longings which weighs so inescapably on Strindberg's creatures is simply an arsenal for Dürrenmatt's characters, from which they can at any time provide themselves with suitable ammunition in the form of 'points' to be scored and barbed remarks to be fired at each other. Round after round is called, each beginning and ending with a gong; all that's missing is a referee to interrupt when blows go beneath the belt and to announce the final winner.

In Strindberg, Kurt, the friend just returned from America, behaves for a long time like a neutral observer – either out of pity or weakness – and acts as catalyst in the contest between Alice and Edgar. In Dürrenmatt, rather than playing the umpire, he quickly joins in the fight with no sign of weakness at all as an equally matched third combatant; in America he has pursued a career as a gangster – a typical Dürrenmatt touch – and now blithely maintains that what goes on in a Strindbergian middle-class marriage is hardly any less criminal than what happens in Chicago: with professional superiority he emerges from the battle the victor. Furthermore, he comes out of it relatively unscathed, while Dürrenmatt's Alice (as opposed to her counterpart in Strindberg) succeeds in over-throwing Edgar and transforming him into a crippled, babbling wreck, yet without freeing herself from him. The struggle must go on; and the hated opponent is also the beloved partner, without whom everything would be finished and done with.

The transformation of a naturalistic play about conflict into a thorough-going, strictly formalised sparring match also has the effect of releasing the actors from the need to present solid characters. Their means of expression are channelled into each phase of the confrontation with the aim of achieving maximum effect (each one intent on 'playing the opponent into the ground'). The characters don't converse; rather they throw quotations at each other – employing the technique of actors in doing so. This emphasis on the technique, on the structure of the contest brings about a release from the con-fines of Strindberg's world, a distancing from it: it becomes a play-world. 'Fate' or 'destiny' are concepts which lose their meaning where the characters – by honouring precise rules of play – are so demonstratively making a game out of their torments: their case is both more grotesque and more grievous.

This middle-class marital hell becomes a waxworks display. Dürrenmatt's arrangement sets the characters free, yet the earlier obligations imposed by destiny are now replaced by the obligation to move (as in chess), the obligation to 'play the game': he who loses his sang-froid and his self-control has already lost. This creates a new catastrophe. For Dürren-matt's characters, who act in scornful cognisance of their position and who endure with apparent equanimity the realis-ation that their life is an evil swamp – for these creatures there is the inescapable catastrophe that it's all theatre, it's all a game to be played.

15

Minna, Urfaust, Titus Andronicus

So vehement and occasionally almost violent was the theatrical activity with which Dürrenmatt occupied the five years between the premières of *The Meteor* and *Portrait of a Planet* that one might sense in it an escape from the rigours of the writing-desk into more enlivening and stimulating practical work. He came to terms with Shakespeare, Strindberg and the German classics as an adapter and he also directed the plays himself; so, by way of practical involvement with unfamiliar material, he developed some new dramaturgical principles of his own. The basis of these adaptations and productions is a cutting and tightening (also a coarsening and heightening) of scenes and dialogue, a continuous reduction to the simplest, most forceful forms of theatrical expression, and a clarification of the way the play moves forward. Seen from the point of view of Dürrenmatt the *author*, whose first adaptations (*King John* and *Play Strindberg*) showed a considerable investment of his own inventive powers, the later pieces are merely skilful hack-jobs: a 'dramaturgical arrangement' of Lessing's *Minna von Barnhelm*, which craftily manipulates the original by means of slight retouching; a stage version of Goethe's *Urfaust*, which fits the 'Sturm und Drang' fragment into the framework of a puppet play; and a *Titus Andronicus* from Shakespeare, which reads as though a rather unimaginative Dürrenmatt disciple had put it together by mechanically following the *King John* recipe.

Dürrenmatt's *Minna von Barnhelm* seems at a brief glance to be a straightforward version of Lessing's text made simply more theatrically effective by slight transpositions, speeded up by the elimination of all the monologues, and shortened by sharpening dialogue exchanges. Deeper down, however, the play has altered perceptibly.

It is always more clearly about money than Lessing's original text, even when the talk is of honour and virtue; Riccaut, who only speaks French in Dürrenmatt's version, has been promoted to director in a Prussian ministry; Just bursts into a tirade of hate against the bloody King and his bloody war, and the Count von Bruchsal, Lessing's rich and benign deus ex machina, turns out to be a penniless scrounger: with these broad, contrived effects Dürrenmatt turns the play against the world and the society which produced it.

There are clearly both aesthetic and financial reasons for the popularity of Goethe's *Urfaust* on the stage today. This stylistically unified, if fragmentary early version whose plot is limited to the Gretchen affair, 'spares' the theatres the expensive and aesthetically difficult ghost scenes (witches' kitchen and Walpurgis Night). Dürrenmatt's conception exploits the laconic brevity, the balladesque economy of the text. On the stage it calls for only the essential props and a rostrum for the actors, which, with a few chairs round it, doubles as a table; he groups around the main actors a 'chorus' of supporting players who assume different functions and supporting roles as required – in this way the *Urfaust*, especially for Dürrenmatt as director, becomes an exercise in 'epic' staging. The great gaps in the action he plugs, much as Brecht did in his adaptation for the Berliner Ensemble, with linking quotations from the chapbook of Dr Faust, and here Mephisto becomes the narrator or master of ceremonies.

But there is one gap in the story which Dürrenmatt does not fill, preferring to base a whimsical interpretation of his own upon it. He concludes from the absence of the scene in which Faust is rejuvenated in the witches' kitchen that the scarcely twenty-year-old Goethe envisaged Faust as an old man and had written the tragedy of 'an old man who seduces a young girl and leaves her holding the baby'. Everything which is known about the young Goethe's intentions and interests contradicts this defiant hypothesis, and perhaps Dürrenmatt's insistence that there is scholarly evidence to support it is just his way of annoying Emil Staiger, the eminent Zurich expert on Goethe, who had used the solemn occasion of a literary prize-giving to pronounce, ex cathedra and in the lofty name of Goethe, damnation upon Dürrenmatt's 'perversities'. Even as a director's gimmick the notion of Faust as an old man is less than fruitful, but it does one thing, it places upon Gretchen the curse of ludicrousness which rests upon the heroine of Wedekind's Gretchen tragedy, *Music (Musik)*.

Titus Adronicus, his second Shakespeare paraphrase, uses the means already employed in *King John* to unmask war and heroism. It is so weak a piece that one almost forgets that it was Peter Brook's *Titus Andronicus* that inspired Dürrenmatt to write *Frank V*, and that in *Romulus the Great* he had already found a witty plot of his own to depict the fall of the Roman Empire.

The story of Titus Andronicus, the stubborn and tyrannical general who brings Tamora, queen of the defeated Goths, to Rome and earns her hatred by executing one of her sons as a sacrifice to his own sons who were among the fallen, and who is then almost destroyed by her as she rises to be the wife of the cruel Emperor Saturninus. The story of the villainous negro, Aaron, Tamora's lover, who induces Tamora's sons to rape and mutilate Titus's daughter and to kill the Emperor's brother while putting the blame on Titus's sons. (Titus even cuts off his own hand in a vain attempt to save them from execution.) Titus Andronicus's cruel revenge when he serves her own sons' flesh up to the queen, baked in a pie. Finally the triumph of Titus Andronicus's son, Lucius, who flees, then returns at the head of an army of Goths to free Rome from the tyranny of Saturninus and Tamora. Dürrenmatt takes over the entire plot, scene by scene, of this bloodthirsty example of early Shakespeare in which thirteen of the fifteen main characters are murdered, complete with all its grisly details, for example the black baby Aaron fathers on Tamora.

Characteristic alterations: Aaron, a prime example of 'amoral nature' eludes revenge and escapes to darkest Africa with his son. ('Thus we become again what once we were, not slaves of Rome, but free cannibals.') Lucius on the other hand, the last of the Romans, is executed by Alaric, Prince of the Goths, when he takes over Rome. Characteristic additions: the cruel Saturninus, like the popular image of Nero, sees himself as a poet and sensitive art-lover; Titus Andronicus, pretending in his insatiable lust for revenge to be mad, organises a street-theatre with war-cripples to perform plays in praise of the state, and is jeered for his pains. ('This response shatters the patriot, insults the artist in me; let us produce well-made, positive plays'!); an exhausted imperial executioner appears and appeals for sympathy ('Just try torturing in this heat! I'm sweating like a pig.') and praises Titus when he hacks off his hand ('nicely done, old man. My respect!')

More crucial than these grotesque embellishments is the rigour with which Dürrenmatt reduces Shakespeare's text, with the exception of a few passages, to bald theatrical situations and laconic exchanges of dialogue. The figures in the play, one of whose main motifs is mutilation and whose grandeur resides in its lament for the pain imposed on the violated flesh, have been subjected to further mutilation, in that Dürrenmatt has stripped them of their capacity to express themselves and hence of their capacity for suffering. Atrocity is piled crudely upon atrocity, and one single dominant theme emerges, senseless bloodshed wrought in the name of justice and the state. Titus Andronicus, a figure who could have stepped from the Old Testament with his righteousness and his faith in justice – 'Rome's greatness is not the sword, but the law with which she rules the world' – abandons his faith in a just world in the face of the gratuitous cruelty of Saturninus and Tamora – 'Only madness can cope with the assurdity of this world' – and runs amok in his lust for revenge – this is another variation of Dürrenmatt's basic theme that in a chaotic world, justice is impossible. Yet this theme only comes through in sententious comments on the atrocities, not in the dialectic of the action, and the play's language and ideas give the impression of having been assembled from ready-made components. They strain after malice, as in Alaric's closing lines.

> What price justice? What price revenge?
> No more than names for dirty tricks!
> The globe of the world trundles through the void,
> And perishes as senselessly, as we all perish
> What is, what was, what will be, all must die.

16

Portrait of a Planet

Dürrenmatt's theatre was, from the beginning, *theatrum mundi*. With the single exception of *The Meteor*, he never dramatised the purely personal experience or fate of the individual. In every play the actions and sufferings of the hero were related to the weal and woe of a town, a petty state or an empire, in short of a community which served as a model for the world; every play dealt essentially with the question of whether this evil, inadequate world could be saved, redeemed, or turned into a just world. The sequence of Dürrenmatt's heroes is a procession of foolhardy moralists who act under the delusion that they can, through violence or self-sacrifice, save the world, and who perish in the face of a world that is by definition amoral.

In *Portrait of a Planet* there no longer are any such heroes, merely shabby caricatures of them, like the failed revolutionary who has been consigned to a lunatic asylum – 'Poverty disappeared, but men were not happy. The new world had not grown any better, nor even more just ... Man had become more free, but his freedom did not set him free. He possessed more than he had ever possessed, but above all he possessed himself. He stood face to face with himself and no longer knew what to do with himself.' – or a grotesque little group of female missionaries trying to convert cannibals to pork, while 'a nation with a civilisation going back three thousand years – is being forced by famine to devour human corpses'. Cannibal dialogue: 'The fact is, we've run out of negroes. – Chinese? – We're right out of them too. – Then I'd rather starve. – We could perhaps round up a few honkies. – They taste terrible. – Animal flesh? – One simply cannot touch animal flesh. – Before, you used to eat animal flesh. – That was transgression. – Then eat bananas.' *Portrait of a Planet* builds up, from a multiplicity of small scenes, the picture of a world, no less, that is without fixed values or a fixed perspective.

In 1955 the participants at the 5th Darmstädter Gespräch received a message from Brecht, virtually a manifesto, in response to a question allegedly put to that theatre conference by Dürrenmatt casting doubt on whether the world of today could be represented in theatrical terms at all. (The printed proceedings of the conference record no such question, and it is not known how Brecht got his information from Darmstadt.) Brecht writes, 'In an age which has the scientific knowledge to alter the world to a point where it almost seems habitable, man can scarcely be presented as a victim or a passive object in an unknown, immutable environment.' The postulate which he then added has since been much quoted, 'Today's world can only be described for today's people as a world which admits of change.'

Dürrenmatt, with his fatalistic vision always presents the world as immutable – the best we can expect is a redistribution of its fixed components – and men as objects, victims of an unknown but fixed world. He resolves the problem of representing this world on the stage by drawing his own conclusions about the nature of theatre in the first instance, and then basing his conclusions about the world on these, so that there is no attempt to transfer a general view of the world to the stage. In this way dramatic theory and technique become tools to help us to understand the world. (*Eine kleine Dramaturgie der Politik, Zur Dramaturgie der Schweiz,* and other essays illustrate this.)

Portrait of a Planet offers a shorthand version, a distillation of the 'whole' world in a 90 minute scenic kaleidoscope – capitalism, colonialism, racism, socialism, terrorism, cannibalism, poverty, drugs, aircraft hijacking, moon landing, Vietnam war, apartheid, communes and promiscuity, consumer fetishism, conceptual art, concentration camps and everything the casual newspaper or magazine reader might recognise as a 'topical issue' comes up in this play. Obviously it tells us nothing about these topics that anybody who occasionally leafs through the papers or magazines wouldn't know, but this is no condemnation of the play. The world here, more than ever, is just something to play with, a stimulus, material for the artist, without inherent value, selected at random and in a sense interchangeable. The problem is a theatrical one, not a problem in the real world; namely how to present the maximum subject matter with the minimum means. The new dramatic technique Dürrenmatt had revealed in *Play*

Strindberg where he reduced the subject to purely theatrical situations and concentrated on play-acting was now put to the test.

The means Dürrenmatt chooses for his extended experiment, his artistic construction, his working model of the world (which obeys its own rules, like chess) are: an empty stage, eight actors, a few costumes, a few props, in short the simplest, crudest, most primitive means, more or less those used for 'street theatre', and the results show that these means are quite adequate for staging the whole world, and a few gods to boot, as a fugue of short sketches with laconic dialogue.

Yet if this ascetic exercise, this sequence of sometimes cabarettistic, sometimes sentimental scenes and sketches seems, even momentarily, to present a picture of the world, it is an illusion, for the entire play presupposes that TV and the news magazines have familiarised us with the world it presents, so that it need only allude to it from scene to scene to produce an infallible 'Aha' of recognition from the audience.

Of course, this survey of the world has not been done for its own sake, there is a grand 'idea' behind it; Dürrenmatt shows us our planet in the final second before its end; behind all these (sometimes intentionally) trivial scenes lies a central event, a cosmic catastrophe which will wipe out the world in a second, the solar explosion. Prologue and epilogue are delivered by four gods who, as representatives of the audience as it were, view the natural spectacle from afar on the Milky Way, and comment on it with a smug, quite human, ignorance. 'A sun. Over there. Going west! – Ah. – When? – Any minute now. – It's turning into a supernova. – A what? – It is disintegrating and its matter is being blasted into space. – Ah. – Varoom! – Eh? – Varoom! – What? – Ker-boom! – Ah.'

With the solar explosion, once again in Dürrenmatt's plays, ill-fortune and disaster strike on a gigantic scale, shaping the ideas and the content of the scenes. The huge flash of the exploding sun becomes the flashbulb of a cosmic camera which takes a final portrait of the world: hence *Portrait of a Planet*. A final general audit. A record of the final state. Eschatology as a photographic technique. The solar explosion is as plausible as it is implausible. It might occur today or it might never happen: or as Dürrenmatt puts it: 'Improbable as my play is, it is also plausible.' The idea and form are quite similar to Ionesco's plague sequence, *Triumph of Death*. A global catastrophe beyond human comprehension or intervention plunges everything into senselessness: 'The end of the world being determined from the beginning, each scene is senseless, often doubly senseless, inasmuch as it is in itself nonsensical. And people are frequently killed in the play, so that we get a dance of death within a dance of death: and it is precisely here that one might ask oneself whether it would not have been tactically shrewder to let a world perish which was still whole, or at least one which held some deeper meaning. However the world we live in is neither whole nor meaningful, but enmeshed in disastrous banalities.'

Both the question, whether it might not have been tactically shrewder, that is theatrically more effective, to create a totally fictitious world, and the answer with its sweeping reference to alleged real and present conditions when in fact Dürrenmatt is only talking about his own view of the world, are quite characteristic of his theorising about the drama. From the fact that the cosmic catastrophe in all its improbability and universality seems a-historical in relation to all human history, Dürrenmatt, in the theoretical preface to the play, draws the final surprising conclusion that his view of the world in this play, in spite of its patent references to here and now, and to topical matters, is, and can only be, a-historical. The earth can only be portrayed eschatologically, in the present. Its disorder can only be demonstrated radically if it is wrenched from its history and its future, if history is no longer accepted as an excuse, nor the future as a ground for hope. With this, Dürrenmatt's world-view becomes a monad.

Portrait of a Planet, half boring, formalistic experiment, half naive, moralising sermon, is not a product of anger but of desperation. Dürrenmatt literally means what he makes Adam say, 'The world is chance.' The play is intended to show us the writing on the wall, and it is the first play in twenty years that he does not call a comedy.

17
The Conformer

Had Dürrenmatt abandoned his world of superlatives, his grand confrontations and his monumental figures once and for all with *Portrait of a Planet*? Did he no longer believe there was any need for the *poetic fable* which he had, in his Schiller lecture, called the mainspring of drama? Those who claimed he had have been proved wrong. Dürrenmatt's recent works seem thin and austere, even dry when compared to the phantasy and teeming new ideas in his earlier plays. They provide little more than a skeleton of dialogue for the actor to flesh out in performance. They are each based on a single premise, they are put together with the calculating coolness of a chess-player, but they still use monumental figures, and they still have plots which are larger than life, and show the struggle for power in a world in which chance, as ever, reigns supreme.

In his *Kleine Dramaturgie der Politik* (1968) Dürrenmatt, with terrifying remoteness from reality, reduces the communist and capitalist systems to two handy board games along the lines of that old favourite, Monopoly. Entire ideologies are broken down into sets of interchangeable pretexts, excuses and alibis for power politicians whose sole preoccupation is the preservation of their own power. His two most recent works read like grim proofs of his mundane thesis – homo homine lupus. In the novella *The Fall* (*Der Sturz*) which was the most succinct example of his 'new dramaturgy' that Dürrenmatt had produced when it appeared in 1971, we are shown a secret session in the Kremlin – intrigues and power-struggles, the fall and assassination of a great dictator, the new party line and the establishment of a new hierarchy – all of this brought about by sheer, ludicrous chance, by error and oversight. 'Tough luck' turned into history with maximum effect, be it only on Dürrenmatt's chessboard.

If the Kremlin setting of *Der Sturz*, a novella which reads, incidentally, like the laconic prose summary of a two-act drama, involved the deliberate use of cliché, so too did the American, capitalist, underworld trappings of *The Conformer*. The 'world' of this play is the major city in a great state under the dictatorship of organised capital. It is a world of supreme simplicity governed by the single principle of total venality, total corruption. Whoever has the most money has the power, and this is in effect the man who has the majority shareholding in the all-powerful chemical corporation, which overrides the pseudo-democratic posturings of whatever puppet-government might seem at any time to be at the helm of the ship of state. Here, just as in Shakespeare's good old histories, or at a more provincial level in *Frank V*, murder is the standard weapon in the power-struggle. The elegant man of the world calls upon the services of a perfectly organised murder syndicate which preserves its monopoly with a strict code of conduct. This arrangement naturally means that the interests of capital and of the underworld become progressively more entangled with one another. It soon ceases to be important who is infiltrating or buying up whom. In the final estimate the power of the state and of gangsterdom are shown to be one and the same. The figures in *The Fall*, and they are flat figures rather than rounded characters, are designated by single letters to underline the abstract, chess-like effect. The ones in *The Conformer* are similarly reduced to single functions and have one syllable names – Doc, Boss, Cop, Ann, Bill, Jack. The play has two acts, but is, as Dürrenmatt himself stresses, really divided into five parts, each opening with a 'story' from one of the five main characters in which he introduces himself to the audience and explains how he got involved in the plot. This starts with Doc, the conformer himself. He was, as he recalls, a biochemist with a distinguished university career behind him who went into the chemical industry for a princely salary and was then made redundant in the *great economic crisis* (which has no further bearing on the play). His spoilt wife ran off and took their son with her, while he eked out an existence as a taxi-driver for several years until he met Boss. – 'By chance. Two years ago. One blood-red winter evening. The tyres of his Cadillac had been slashed. His Rolls was riddled with bullet-holes, his Buick had been hijacked by a rival gang. So he had to take a taxi. My taxi.' – The fateful stroke of chance is shown in flashback, a car-chase punctuated with macabre, comic, gangster-movie dialogue, in which Doc gives Boss's rivals, Wasserkopf-Abraham and Jeff of the Wolfpack Gang, the slip. The pair get into conversation and it transpires that Doc is just the man to find a perfect solution for the murder syndicate's main problem, disposing of corpses. He works out a technical application of certain basic facts of organic chemistry and invents the necrodialysator, an apparatus for dissolving corpses. For a year he has been living in an underground laboratory (in which the play is set), where the syndicate delivers corpses and he disposes of them without trace. This gives him a key position and makes him Boss's closest confidant.

The basic premise is almost ludicrous in its improbability, since 'in reality' it is unlikely that any customer giving a contract to a murder syndicate would want the victim to disappear without trace. On the contrary he would want a neat, readily identifiable corpse, without which, if it were, say, a matter of inheritance, he would only come into the money after the victim's absence had been reported and he had then been officially listed as a missing person and eventually declared legally dead, which would take years. Of course Dürrenmatt would dismiss any argument against his fiction which was based on mere probability. It is clear that the important thing for him was to expose the corrupt natural sciences yet again, twelve years after *The Physicists*, as the stooges of criminals in power, even if it meant overdoing it. Biochemistry was fashionable, so he made his scientist a biochemist, probably with Jacques Monod in mind, who had provided corroboration for Dürrenmatt's blind, fatalistic world-view in his philosophical best-seller which interpreted creation as chance. The function of the scientist (to whom we owe essential discoveries about life) in a negative piece like this must logically be purely negative, destructive and deadly, and if Doc, as might have been a shade more plausible, had made himself indispensable to the syndicate by inventing a biochemical method of murder which forensic science could not detect, the play would have lacked an element of its macabre theatrical effect, namely the continuous, accelerating flow of corpses for processing which lent an accent of its own to the successive scenes.

Scene one. Boss visits Doc and reports that a mysterious blackmailer is trying to penetrate the syndicate. They wait for him together, and we get some melancholy small talk from the aging gangsters.

BOSS. Business worries. Dicky ticker. Dizzy spells. Swollen ankles. A word of advice, Doc – keep your hands off the women. These last two years, I've been living with a moll.

DOC. You're always on about that.

BOSS. I set her up in a very expensive apartment.

DOC. And every day you begrudge it more and more.

BOSS. It's the jealousy. It's killing me.

DOC. Leave that to your rivals.

BOSS. I don't even know with whom she's deceiving me with.

DOC. Put a private eye on her.

BOSS. I have my pride.

DOC. You didn't use to be so proud.

BOSS. I didn't use to be so old.

DOC. Go and see a psychiatrist.

BOSS. I've been through all that. Defective relationship with the mother.

The mysterious stranger appears. It is Cop, the Chief of Police. He knows all about the syndicate's activities and demands a cut. Fifty per cent.

BOSS. This undertaking is my whole life's work.

COP. You organised the biggest gang of assassins in the annals of our community.

BOSS And you organised the biggest corruption racket in the annals of our community.

COP. The pot calling the kettle black.

BOSS. You want to ruin me.

COP. If I wanted to ruin you, I would simply liquidate you.

(The play's entire dialogue is couched in this curt, hard-boiled, telegrammese, and, in German, the consistent misuse of the imperfect has almost reached the point of self parody with Dürrenmatt. Boss laments, but accepts Cop's demands, even when, on top of Cop's fifty per cent, Doc is given twenty per cent, for which he ('the intellectual of us three') is to deal directly with the customers in place of the sales manager whom Cop has liquidated. Doc is to force prices up steeply.

Part two, enter the beautiful Ann.
I'm Boss's mistress.

I was a photographic model once, nothing famous . . . He spoils me. I drive an expensive sports car. He showers me with jewels and fur coats. The latest thing he gave me was a small Rembrandt, only I haven't to show it to anybody.

Then she comes to her confession. A couple of months ago she dropped into a bar by chance, and asked a total stranger to sleep with her.

Maybe because I wanted to get my own back on Boss. Maybe because I was ashamed of myself for not holding out against Boss.

This stranger chanced to be Doc. 'It was very wonderful.' Since then Ann has been Doc's mistress – but she doesn't know what he does for a living, and he only mutters vaguely about industrial diamonds. He doesn't know that she is the 'moll' Boss is always talking about.

Since Ann doesn't mention any names Doc has no way of knowing who her lover is, and he for his part doesn't even mention that he knows Boss, far less what their relationship is. They decide together that Ann will leave her lover for good the next day. Doc will get her to a safe hide-out and they will start a 'new life' at an unspecified date in the future.

Ann leaves, Doc goes into the next room and Bill enters, a twenty-four-year-old student who has switched from biology to sociology. He introduces himself like every other character in the play with sweeping confessions and wide knowledge. Bill is an anarchist.

It is indecent to occupy one's thoughts with atoms, molecules, spiral nebulae or the carbon compounds when a corrupt state, an even more corrupt society or some imbecile dogma or other is bent on annihilating the world . . . Revolutions and their tremendous sacrifices create only further compulsions to alter the world yet again. It is useless to keep on inventing new ideologies, constructing new utopias. There's been enough argument and discussion. Only a greater necessity can bring humanity to its senses, yet absurd solutions are a natural part of an absurd world. Our struggle is directed against every political system and against every form of society. There can be no half measures. Our aim is not to fight corruption, but to encourage it. A cleverly-planted time-bomb is reality, not utopia. Railway points wrongly switched at the right moment is not an ideological matter, but a meaningful manipulation of the course of history. Non-action is bad. Conformity is criminal. Plotting is a waste of time. Only violence can be of any help.

When Bill hears a noise he hides and eavesdrops on the conversation when the first customer arrives to negotiate a murder with Doc. It is Jack, the son of Nick, the owner of the chemical works, who has just died. Nick wants his stepbrother, Bill, bumped off.

The chemical works were founded by my grandfather. I cannot possibly allow the family business to fall into the hands of a person whose origins are really unmentionable. His mother slept around with anyone who'd have her – and in old Nick's own bed. His father hit the bottle. The son was bequeathed the controlling interest in the shares. He became the president of the board of directors, and the richest man in the country. We've got to put an end to this scandalous situation.

Jack offers a hundred thousand for the hit, but Doc demands a million. 'I charge customers according to what I think the market can stand.' Jack goes off to get the board of directors to release the money.

As soon as Jack has gone Bill comes out. Doc and Bill recognise each other at first sight, they are father and son, or more exactly, as Doc formulates it, 'I happen to be your father, and you happen to be my son.' His mother 'slept around with anyone who'd have her', until she finally died in an air crash with her latest husband, Nick, the head of the chemical works. Doc realises that Bill is the hated step-brother, the sole heir whose murder he has just been negotiating with Jack. He suggests to Bill that for two million he will have

Jack bumped off instead, but Bill is not interested. He has an entirely different proposition, for ten million; the assassination of the President.

> I belong to the most way-out anarchist group ever known ... I hope to come to an understanding with your organisation, I shall commission it to eradicate first one, then the other president ... I shall blow the world sky-high, and with it the colossal shit-heap of profits I made from the chemical works.

Doc doubts whether the syndicate will take the contract, and wonders whether personal initiatives of this order make political sense. There is a final grand, heart-to-heart discussion before the two part with their differences unresolved.

BILL. With my millions, all we have to do is to make practical application of your scientific knowledge.

DOC. Knowledge has nothing to do with politics.

BILL. Maybe it has. If you make a mixture of methane, water vapour, ammonia and hydrogen, and subject it to an electric current, you obtain amino acid, the raw material of life itself. That was the experiment that made you famous. I am simply repeating it in the field of politics. The mixture is our society. Ammonia and methane are peculiarly pungent gases, and the electric spark is my millions, with which I work through you.

DOC. But what's all this to do with me?

BILL. It is to you I owe all my convictions. To you and to your destiny as a man, as a scientist.

DOC. My destiny is without importance.

BILL. Everyone owes his development to one experience.

DOC. You want to avenge what happened to – my destiny?

BILL. Honour thy father and thy mother. When the chemical works fired you, I began to think deeply about how our society is organised, the social structure which this economic crisis exposed. And when my mother began sleeping with Old Nick, I began to study how to destroy this world that had destroyed you.

DOC. You cannot avenge me, because I long ago got my own

revenge. On myself. Like a deceived husband who takes his
revenge by castrating himself.

BILL. The world no longer matters to you. It just provides you
with your carcases. It is not I who am annihilating the
world, it is the world that is annihilating itself. I am simply
giving it a helping hand.

The fourth figure to offer his personal confessions to the
audience is Boss, and he has the body of Ann brought on for
the occasion. He has strangled her, not out of jealousy but
for tactical reasons – he wants to put moral pressure on Doc
who is getting too powerful for his liking.

Because he had this bad conscience. Same as all intellectuals.
They see the world in two ways simultaneously: the world as it
is, and the world as it ought to be. They get their living from
the world as it is. From the world as it ought to be they derive
their standards by which they judge the world they live off, and
as long as they cultivate a sense of guilt they feel they are ab-
solved – I soon got wise to that kind of humbug. Those high-
minded scum are unfitted for power-struggles. They revel in
their guilt complexes. They even feel themselves responsible
for the creation of the world, as Doc does, yet his consciousness
of guilt is mere fantasy, a luxury the poor dope allows himself in
order to shirk realities. Good old Doc! He's going to have an
orgy of guilt about Ann's murder. But then in the end out of
fear of revenge he'll come round to my way of thinking. He'll
shift his allegiance from Cop and back to me, then with an even
worse conscience than before he'll make the best of a bad job.

Doc comes on, and Boss makes a last effort to impose his
own business principles, no politics and reasonable prices, in
place of the new course Cop has proposed for the syndicate,
but Doc has already gone over to the side of the new man in
power, and they have already agreed to take on the assassination
of the President. Boss now brings out the body of Ann, which
he has been concealing, but Doc betrays no sign of emotion at
the sight of the corpse of the woman on whom he had pinned

all his hopes for the future, though he is inwardly on the point of collapse when he recognises her. Giving nothing away, he shoves Ann into the necrodialysator – 'I never knew her.'

This proves him to be the complete conformer whom you can use at will. He even gives up his percentage and keeps only five thousand a month, on condition that Boss approves the assassination of the President. 'My collaboration in this organisation has got to have some deeper significance.'

Cop is the last figure to come on and tell the audience his story, and here Dürrenmatt once again takes up the motif of the lifelong relationship of amicable hostility between the master crook and the great lawman. He had used it in his first novel, *The Judge and his Hangman*, and had later elaborated it on a grander scale in *The Marriage of Mr Mississippi*. By now, however, Dürrenmatt's world has become so gloomy and hermetic that not even a just man can finally believe in the triumph of good and the salvation of the world. Cop, who has followed Boss's criminal activities since he, as a young policeman, was shot and crippled by Boss who was then a young burglar, no longer wants revenge or justice, now that he is in sight of his goal.

> When I finally decided to swoop down on Boss and turn his organisation into a nest of squealing rats, circumstances forced me to the unhappy realisation – not all of a sudden, but (what was even worse) step by painful step – that I, a crippled wreck, a rotten lump of flesh on the path to damnation, that I was alone the guilty one, for the simple reason that I alone, in the world where justice can be bought and sold, was seeking real, absolute justice.

All he wants is for his death to have some meaning.

Cop appears in the underground laboratory and brings the body of Boss whom he has liquidated on the instructions of the District Attorney and the Mayor, for the state's own

officials have now moved into the syndicate. 'Good old Boss
... he never could grasp that the golden days of private
enterprise are finished. Thousands like him are suffering the
same fate. Big game hunting.' Now the bodies of Jack and
Bill are delivered. Jack has been bumped off for 'technical
reasons' (a cynic might say to tie off a loose end in the plot),
Bill because his anarchism was just too right for the world. –
'The D.A. and the Supreme Court Judge were captivated by
this young man. He was a conformer, though, without
realising it.' – But Cop has not finished his confession yet. The
ridiculous old servant of justice has committed both these
murders off his own bat, without instructions from the organisation, and in so doing he has, as he sees it, put Bill's anarchic
principles into practice, for he has not taken a fee from either
of them. 'Only the collapse of giant firms can have any effect
on this world. Then the shit will really hit the fan.' Cop also
knows that Sam and Jim, the syndicate's hit-men, will kill him
for this.

> Now, whatever Sam and Jim are going to do with me, it will be
> just, even though it may be a pitiable kind of justice. But these
> days any kind of justice at all is too much to hope for ... But
> for a brief second in eternity I held in check the fatal prolifer-
> ation of your activities. Why? In the end one somehow has to
> retain one's own self-respect ...'

Cop tries several times in this scene to get Doc to confess
that he is Bill's father, but Doc denies his dead son, just as he
has denied his dead mistress, Ann, and when Cop tells him
that the organisation is looking for Bill's father who is now
the sole heir to the chemical firm and the richest man in the
country, Doc's denial becomes final. 'Jack's widow is offer-
ing ten million for his head ... So that she can inherit the
biggest fortune in the country.' Cop gives Doc Bill's wallet,
in which he had found a photo of Bill's father, so he has
known all along that Doc was the man they were looking for.

Sam and Jim, the hit-men, appear and bump off Cop who takes his end with laconic pathos, 'Funny how life suddenly has some meaning . . . When you kick the bucket you kick conforming too.' They then strip Bill's body as it lies there, and finally they beat up Doc who, in mortal panic, has already destroyed the photo from Bill's wallet, the last proof of his identity, and force him to hand over most of his income to them. He continues to do the dirty work for a measly five hundred. 'We need his brains.' This final twist – not the worst possible, but the most fatalistic – was only added to the play, whose first draft dates from 1959, shortly before the first performance in the spring of 1973. Doc obliterates all traces of his own identity and sinks into totally anonymous, totally hopeless conformism for bare survival.

The quotations make any interpretation of the comedy superfluous. It is absolutely transparent and it provides a running commentary on itself. It is a logical continuation of Dürrenmatt's later work, a monomanic phantasy of consider-able formal bravura, a piece of cold and empty virtuosity which goes out for its effects with careless abandon. It relates to nothing outside itself, and anything in it which might con-ceivably relate to experience, or psychology, or reality or any kind of actual problem is in fact used as a mere counter in an encapsulated intellectual game, which deploys them with the same tasteless indifference, with which Doc disposes of the bodies that come along in his necrodialysator. It tells us nothing about the nature of power, or about those who wield power, nothing about their fears and obsessions, nothing about the fragility of the capitalist pecking order, not even anything about chance as a factor in history. All this play tells us is what kind of intellectual game amuses Dürrenmatt, what kind of motifs and constellations he favours, and what strategies he employs to work them out. It shows us that he is still the master, still as brilliant as ever, and that these games still amuse him – even if they don't amuse anybody else. He is not too different from old Doc with his moloch-machine as he processes material from the world into pure theatre.

18

Dürrenmatt's Work on the Stage

Dürrenmatt's plays are not intended as literature, but as theatre: it is not until rehearsals that the text reaches its final form (that is, final as far as the given production is concerned). The script is a score and may be revised for each production since different situations will require different solutions. Dürrenmatt stresses that the material with which a playwright works is not the word but the stage. It is *'always the author's teacher, he can always learn from it. The main problem is to distinguish between the writer's and the theatre's prerogatives.'* The word is only the *'outer skin'* of a play: the decisive factor is not its absolute poetic quality but its pregnancy, its effectiveness: *'The stage puts a play to the test.'*

The nature of Dürrenmatt's stage directions reveal the growing determination with which he interprets drama as an *'empirical profession'*. In *It is Written* they sound visionary, hardly related to the practicalities of the theatre, often totally unrealisable; in the later plays they become more and more concrete, detailed notes are added to them, and, obviously as the result of bitter experience, Dürrenmatt increasingly limits the director's scope. Even the text of *The Physicists* permits hardly any variations or original ideas to be contributed by the director; and the latest printed work – the Bochum version of *Frank V* – is not far short of being a complete prompt-book. Dürrenmatt resolutely insists: '*The two most important tasks of the director consist, externally, of telling a story on the stage in a lucid and interesting fashion and, internally, of explaining to an actor why in a given situation he must speak certain lines . . . If the foreground which I provide is played properly, then the background will take care of itself.*'

Dürrenmatt has collaborated on the first performances of all his plays. During rehearsals ('*Many problems can only be solved on stage, not from behind a desk*') the texts have taken the form in which they have subsequently been printed. The following extracts from reviews are meant to give an impression on the one hand of the three most important premières – those which have been 'authenticated' by the collaboration of the author – and on the other hand of three famous non-German productions (in Milan, New York and London) which sought and found their own solutions – which were not in every case approved by Dürrenmatt. (For the English edition of this book a brief record of the English productions of *The Meteor*, *Play Strindberg*, and *The Conformer* have also been added.)

THE MARRIAGE OF MR MISSISSIPPI (*Munich*)

First produced on 26th March 1952 at the Munich Kammerspiele. Director: Hans Schweikart; designer: Wolfgang Znamenacek; music: Karl von Feilitzsch. *Anastasia*: Maria Nicklisch; *Mississippi*: Friedrich Domin; *Übelohe*: Peter Lühr; *Saint-Claude*: Wilfried Seyferth; *Diego*: Charles Regnier.

The birth of this play was difficult; Dürrenmatt for once had let his inspiration have full rein ('*I wrote myself again and again into areas which repeatedly necessitated new plans. The work was exciting; those who could see what was going on shook their heads*'). After two years' work there were six different versions, which looked more or less unactable and it was only in Munich that the text for the première was finalised. Dürrenmatt's foreword for the printed version acknowledged Schweikart's collaboration in re-working the play: '*The text of this printed edition follows in large measure that of the first performance which was staged on 26th March 1952 under the direction of Hans Schweikart at the Munich Kammerspiele. Significant elements of the adaptation he made for staging are incorporated. His tendency towards abstraction – for instance, Anastasia's bell never actually made a sound, people always smoked unlighted cigarettes, the servant-girl always wore the same smile – coincides with the author's intentions.*'

In order not to surprise or shock the audience but instead 'to lead them up the garden path' (which Dürrenmatt also enjoys), Schweikart began the play as a parody of a drawing-room drama. Beginning with pace and crisp repartee, he only gradually built up a monstrous grotesqueness. 'Incidents, characters and conversation are hounded out of the realm of psychology into that of parody' (Erich Kästner); 'he pulls out all the stops suggested by the author, sets the searchlights playing, the loudspeakers roaring, the firecrackers exploding. Characters climb through the windows, chat to the audience, explain their function and the author's intentions. Placards float down from the flies and are elucidated' (H. H. Kirst).

Schweikart's characters, made up to look as if they are wearing masks, 'grow' to a certain extent, the more they reveal themselves. This production, deliberately intent on sounding 'wrong notes' and creating unsuitable impressions, was possible because Schweikart had at his disposal a company which was in the main familiar with the psychologically realistic style of theatre: actors who could put across this style with virtuoso skill. (Thus even the apparently unactable part of Anastasia became a 'rôle'.) 'What might have been an irredeemable failure because of a feeble presentation of the grotesque elements, here became a triumph of equilibrium over all the forces of gravity and of usage' (Hanns Braun).

Friedrich Domin in particular – 'the brooding, sallow-faced Public Prosecutor, still impressive even in the shattered condition of the persecuted, and philosophically precise' (Hanns Braun) – made it plain that parody is not achieved by an actor's making fun of a role, but rather by his taking it perfectly and abysmally seriously. 'As a black-coated Mr Mississippi, Domin portrayed a homogeneous character, consistent even to the positioning of his fingertips, for all his rigidity, allowing us to sense his essential humanity as well as his essential quixoticism. His delivery was masterly, with astonishing subtlety' (Bruno E. Werner).

Wilfried Seyferth as Saint-Claude – the foremost counterpart to the ice-cold smoothness affected by the Minister – achieved, 'with his incomparable intellectual vitality, the tension between outer calmness and inner dynamism. The voluptuously sprawling way he sits down for the first time is a memory to cherish' (Bruno E. Werner). 'In contrast to this heavyweight with his leather Kommissar's suit and his fanatical faith in an earthly Utopia, Charles Regnier's bald-headed dandy of a Minister comes across as an epitome of purely self-willed cynicism' (Hanns Braun).

Peter Lühr – 'a wildly agitated marionette with twitching limbs and trembling voice' (H. H. Kirst) – had to achieve a certain truth over and above the melodramatic exaltations, to make the audience feel his genuine despair through all the exaggeratedly theatrical manifestations of suffering: 'As is his way, he went to the extreme; he allowed this quavering bag of nerves returning home from the tropics no sympton of a bodily or a spiritual defect; he dived head first into disgraceful absurdity. And yet how skilfully he brought the human aspect of the character back from the brink of disintegration, so that one believed in his loving and in love itself, the only hope of this world' (Hanns Braun).

Maria Nicklisch, gentle, nervous (certainly far removed from the slowly disappearing species of actress known as the 'society lady', which is strongly re-evoked in the character of Anastasia), kept herself in the centre of this round-dance, not by overbearing power but, with 'wispy red hair framing a pale, usually mournfully inquisitive face' (Hanns Braun), by being very gentle, 'a creature made of glass, brittle and transparent, delicate, seemingly in danger of shattering. Yet her bright fluttering voice can radiate soft inflexible energy' (H. H. Kirst). 'Hardly ever passionately aroused, obediently fulfilling every function required of her, but wreaking revenge quite coolly, killing quite unscrupulously, ultimately unassailable, and totally inscrutable – at the end of the play she wears a ghost-like red evening dress, like a phantom in a flowing sheet, a distant relative of the great apocalyptic whore' (Hanns Braun).

Schweikart's *'tendency towards abstraction'* had been enthusiastically accepted by Dürrenmatt; but five years later he notes: *'Many productions, no doubt misled by the text, have made the mistake of using scenery that was too abstract,'* and demands that the room must *'at the beginning be as real as possible. Only so will it be able to disintegrate.'* Real does not mean realistic. The printed text of 1952 suggests a room *'in which the lines of perspective diverge as they travel upwards, creating a richly absurd effect, as if one were at the bottom of an infernal funnel, as if the room had been built for giants at the top and for dwarves at the bottom'*. This sort of thing is impracticable. Wolfgang Znamenacek, the designer of the Munich première, used quite different methods to create a visual equivalent of the exaggerated style of the text: to set against the play's non-bourgeois action and ideas, he brought in a pile of things which very much conformed to bourgeois artistic taste. 'A transparent setting with a Biedermeier table, Louis XVI chairs and a Venus de Milo in the foreground; crude street singers' pictures unrolling from the flies and in the background the clock-face of Big Ben, skyscrapers, Picasso's "Portrait of a Lady with a Dove", an apple tree and other nonsense. It was as if surrealism had developed its own version of the style of Hans Makart' [the 19th-century historical painter] (Bruno E. Werner).

THE VISIT (*Zürich*)

First produced on 29th January 1956 at the Zürich Schauspielhaus. Director: Oskar Wälterlin; designer: Teo Otto; music: Rolf Langnese. *Claire Zachanassian*: Therese Giehse; *Ill*: Gustav Knuth; *Mayor*: Carl Kuhlmann; *Schoolmaster*: Hanns Krassnitzer; *Priest*: Heinz Woester; *Policeman*: Siegfrit Steiner; *Butler*: Hermann Wlach.

At the beginning the scenery is light, colourful, and bright but as each Act unfolds everything gets gradually more sombre. There are no solid structures to fill and delimit the available space – instead a few fragmented pieces, mobile and often transparent, hanging from the flies, suggesting the location by means of a few realistic details; the whole setting symbolic, pared down to essentials. The overall picture, 'with toy buildings and chimneys set high on a dark background', gives 'theatrical expression to the chimeric nature of the commercial "boom" ' (Erich Franzen). The production elaborates the central theme of the play; the minor characters are handled with discretion, not blown up into caricatures, the citizens of Guellen appear as a collective unit in sometimes extremely stylised arrangements. Wälterlin repressed the satirical elements but exploits Dürrenmatt's theatrical ideas with ease – the Guelleners as 'living trees', the car ride on four chairs. (Dürrenmatt has twice produced the play himself: in 1956 in Basle with gaudy, superabundant theatricality – in the last Act a real car came on stage; and in 1959 in Bern with only the most essential props and with black and white projections, emphasising the play as a cool drama of dialogue).

'The director, Oskar Wälterlin, who in his introductory lecture admitted the play's larger-than-life truthfulness, stressed the undertone of moral pathos rather too sharply. Because of this the "cabaret" scenes which Dürrenmatt sprinkles liberally through the play lost their point completely and the play as a whole became too heavy' (Erich Franzen). Wälterlin shifts the guilt-atonement drama between Ill and Claire Zachanassian firmly into the central position.

Gustav Knuth – an actor who finds it almost impossible to convey an air of unpleasantness – plays Ill as a sturdy, slightly too ponderous representative of middle class virtue, not characterless, just thoughtless: at first jovial and rather pompous, conceited but quite relaxed, lacking in acuteness (even in his conversation with the Mayor), humble, basically naive. 'Only rarely does he allow the sordid shallowness of the character to come to the surface. And when he finally capitulates he does even that with manliness and grace. He has the fear of the courageous man, a fear which because it is rather simple and unimaginative is all the more inspiring of sympathy. Does the sympathy which he stirs in the hearts of the audience endanger the overall effect of the play?' (Elisabeth Brock-Sulzer).

'In keeping with the spirit of Wälterlin's production, Therese Giehse played the multi-millionairess with mask-like immobility. Red-haired, and with chalky-white make-up, she resembled a diamond-studded Fury. All the contrasts inherent in this boldly exaggerated character came across most effectively because of Giehse's superb command of the language' (Erich Franzen). 'She is just as imperious, as ladylike, as god-like, as wild, as shrewd in a masculine way and as mad in a feminine way as the rôle demands' (Elisabeth Brock-Sulzer). 'She has only one single, eerily penetrating tone that sounds frozen: she does not even reveal her inner self when, now that he is cleansed of his sins, she sinks down beside the bier of the murdered Ill to kiss him, as Salome once did' (Siegfried Melchinger).

THE VISIT (*New York*)

Produced: 5th May 1958 at the Lunt-Fontanne Theatre, New York. Director: Peter Brook; designer: Teo Otto; translation and adaptation: Maurice Valency. *Claire Zachanassian*: Lynn Fontanne; *Ill*: Alfred Lunt; *Mayor*: Eric Porter; *Schoolmaster*; Peter Woodthorpe; *Priest*: William Hansen; *Policeman*: John Randolph; *Butler*: John Wyse.

Richard Watts wrote of his suspicion that Maurice Valency's adaptation moderated the play's bold eccentricity, but he praised the colour and liveliness of the production, which he considered Peter Brook had turned into a triumph of theatrical theatre. The Broadway version is rather more austere than the original, with some of the macabre details cut out – for instance: we are spared Claire's artificial limbs and her change of husband from act to act, and the eunuchs have become blind men. However, in comparison with the Hollywood version filmed by Bernhard Wicki, it is not a distorted watering down. The production's sensational success with the New York audience was due not least to the fact that two of the most popular stars of the entertainment business had selected this play with which to launch their own theatre. 'The triumph of the evening is the acting of our two most illustrious drawing-room comedians in the harshest rôles they have played in a quarter of a century' (Brooks Atkinson).

Within the framework of Teo Otto's settings – a somewhat bigger and more opulent version of the Zürich production – Brook stages strongly choreographic ensemble scenes on the one hand (partly with musical accompaniment); and on the other hand he sets Claire and Ill (who in this version is called Anton Schill) in the centre of a sharply defined comedy of types. 'As the village burgomaster, Eric Porter gives a remarkably effective performance, his bluff good humour drifting off into sanctimonious evil at the end' (Brooks Atkinson).

In Brook's production Claire is not excessively snobbish, not monumentally vulgar, but unshakeably lady-like and aristocratic. Ill – by way of contrast – is at the beginning arrogantly complacent and rather disagreeable (which ensures that the audience's sympathy is transferred only very slowly from her to him). 'Mr Lunt . . . hitches up his sluggish suspenders, grins feebly over his soiled and tieless shirt, picks his nose while he continues to hope, and gives us little to go on by way of sympathy for awhile. The sympathy comes at last . . . as he engages in a futile and terrifying ballet of escape on a railway platform, as he achieves a crushed but clear-eyed dignity in his willingness to die. . . .

'Lynn Fontanne's regal, tight-lipped smile is familiar. What is new is almost unspoken, an inexplicable hatred that seems to eat itself alive and thrive on the nourishment as Miss Fontanne listens glassily to every plea that might save Mr Lunt, as she languidly exhales snowdrifts of cigar-smoke while listening to a foolish rhapsody, as she fixes her eyes on a raised rifle and coolly, imperiously talks it and its owner down. The malice is alive, implacable even when it is invisible, a source of enormous, chillingly felt, strength . . . Something of the appalling fascination that seeps through the playhouse is due to director Peter Brook's manipulation of abandoned figures in constantly constricting space. The idle, silky, subtly threatening movements of presumably innocent townsfolk as they halt their man's escape by night, the terror of a line of stubborn backs blocking his every turn, the infinitely slow and quiet encircling that ends in a most discreet murder – all are images of insinuating power' (Walter Kerr).

THE VISIT (*Milan*)

Produced on 31st January 1960 at the Piccolo Teatro, Milan. Director: Giorgio Strehler; designer: Luciano Damiani.

Claire Zachanassian: Sarah Ferrati; *Ill*: Tino Carraro; *Mayor*: Tino Buazelli; *Schoolmaster*: Enzo Tarascio; *Priest*: Andrea Mateuzzi.

Most reviews talk of a 'tragedy'. For Strehler, Dürrenmatt is not a 'conscious Nestroy'. Strehler's way of analysing motives and of examining the mechanism behind even the most frivolous play leaves no room for theatricalism (however well justified), for superficial effects. For him there are no Guelleners playing at being trees in the forest scenes, no deviation from the precise development of the themes, which alone legitimise everything which takes place on stage. He moves Dürrenmatt in the direction of Brecht with a cool, light setting which is purged of all elements of fantasy.

Surprisingly – although it doubtless would have been in accordance with Dürrenmatt's intentions – Strehler did not assimilate the story, did not transpose it into an Italian milieu (perhaps because the figure of the incredibly rich, kinky old lady returning from the legendary land of America is almost too familiar an archetype in post-war Italian literature). The scenery and the thoughtful acting create a dry, specifically Swiss atmosphere: the distance thus produced is meant to hold back purely emotional participation and to facilitate criticism on the part of the audience.

There is hardly one concrete description of Strehler's work on this play in existence: Italian theatre criticism is so political that it judges a production not primarily according to its quality but according to its political purpose. Thus, not only is an anti-capitalist but even an anti-American attitude read into the play. This is welcomed by one set of critics; while the other set disapproves of 'the far too strongly emphasised and frequently hackneyed caricaturing of the world, of which Claire is queen', and in order to be able to praise Strehler nevertheless, they retire into the realm of pure aesthetics – 'The production, far too rambling in the first Act, far too tumultuous in the second, is all the more triumphant in the

third, a masterpiece of expression, rhythm and composition'
(*24 Ore*) – and in the 'extremely precise, extremely suggestive,
extremely impressive production' they see 'the myth of
Strehler's magic' confirmed (*Cronaca di Milano*). The critic
who comes closest to appreciating Strehler's intentions is
Guiseppe Bartolucci, who defends the production (about
which Dürrenmatt himself was sceptical) against the play:
'There is a path which Strehler has been following for years
with persistence, sensibility and with the sort of talent that is
specific to a European director. Judge him as you will: it is the
path of "Reason", which "objectifies" and refines the text
and subordinates the play completely to the function of con-
vincing the audience rationally. It seems to me that here, too,
Strehler has consciously set out along this path: he reconstrues
the motives of Dürrenmatt's tragedy. This leads to a cool,
well-calculated production, whose whole tension derives from
how justice will deal with the conflict between Ill's body and
Claire's desire for vengeance. The production also lays the
greatest stress on the grotesque, quite unconventional contrast
between the evil which produces wealth and the happiness
which stems from misery. Thus Strehler has thoroughly
plausibly resolved to place more emphasis on the rational
Dürrenmatt and less on the bizarre. This has led him to force
the stylistic and theatrical characteristics of the author into
the background, to leave the way clear for the essence of the
tragedy to come through. Beda Allemann has pointed out that
the individual threads of the action in the three Acts run
parallel, as it were, each one self-contained, each one thematically striving to reach its own goal with characters who,
lacking in psychology, reveal step by step what determines
their behaviour and what prevails over them. This slows
down the rhythm, creates room for reasoning dialogue, renders impossible any unconnected fabrications, and on the
other hand permits, as Strehler has done, the stretching to the
limit of the "Cartesian" curve of these motives which deter-

mine people's behaviour, and allows the eclectic diversity of
Dürrenmatt's political and social commitment to be brought
to a head.

'In this sense Strehler has worked miracles: for example, he
displayed a skilful touch in the elimination of all the Wilder-
like lyrical digressions, in the weeding out of all the non-
committal and romantically superfluous features which have
made the author so popular on the European stage. The
significant number of such conventional effects he has removed from the far from homogeneous text is something
which even the unsuspecting spectator is bound to notice:
Strehler underlines for example the element of "Americanisa-
tion" in the arrival of the vengeful Claire and, by linking
visual elements from a certain type of American film with
symbols from a specifically Western European psychology,
he removes the possibility of its seeming pure coincidence of
simple economic contingencies. Opposed to this there is, in
happiness as well as in unhappiness, the poverty of a Swiss
provincial town, which Dürrenmatt no doubt saw as a
mystifying parody on hypocrisy and evil, and which Strehler
reinterprets as religious mendacity, arrogance and soulless-
ness.

'One can see, for example, the degree of studied evil-
mindedness he has brought out in Sarah Ferrati in a rôle
which is in fact taciturn but highly suggestive: Claire Zachanassian, paradoxical Medea of a tragedy which has set money
in the place of God, extremely unconventional in her desire
to bury her first love in a grave beneath the Mediterranean
sun – very much alive, but with a heart which has turned to
stone. And the others: Tino Carraro, agonizedly trying to
understand the changed consciousness of his fellow-citizens,
their striving for their own wealth and his downfall; Tino
Buazelli, the benevolently pompous and fundamentally hard-
hearted Mayor; Enzo Tarascio, the Schoolmaster, who at
first refuses to believe that there is so much evil but who then

becomes a hypocritical advocate of a crime committed in the name of virtue; finally, Andrea Matteuzzi, the Priest, who treats the poor Ill with merciless amiability. The long, fairly slow dialogue between Claire and Ill in the third Act is the best example of how Strehler has de-theatricalised this text and brought out the essential notes, with which he, as dramaturg and director has clarified the work, made it more precise and sharpened it.'

THE PHYSICISTS (*Zürich*)

First produced on 20th February 1962 at the Zürich Schauspielhaus. Director: Kurt Horwitz; designer: Teo Otto; *Fräulein Doktor Mathilde von Zahnd*: Therese Giehse; *Möbius*: Hans Christian Blech; *Newton*: Gustav Knuth; *Einstein*: Theo Lingen; *Monika*: Hanne Hiob; *Voss*: Fred Tanner.

The production of *The Physicists* by Horwitz, a model of discreet directing, wholly true to the play, is rather deliberate, and relies absolutely on the text. Even Teo Otto's set, 'both sinister and conventional (Elisabeth Brock-Sulzer), keeps in every detail to Dürrenmatt's instructions (or, alternatively, Dürrenmatt gives a precise description of Otto's scenery – for the printed text 'documents' this production). Horwitz concentrates with extreme care on guiding the actors and directing the dialogue. 'The characters, which are constructed as types, are interpreted psychologically' (Ernst Schumacher).

'Light of step, Gustav Knuth glides out of his cell into the room: he is dressed as Newton in a white wig and a colourful, shimmering silk coat. He plays the scholar with cunning roguery, with childlike naivety, with the gestures of a half-modest, half-coquettish girl, and momentarily also with the air of a naughty child, when his leg lands unawares on the silk sofa. A constant smirk plays over his face. His wig serves as his method of unmasking himself, he tears it from his head when he confesses his true identity' (Irma Voser).

'Theo Lingen as Einstein (dishevelled hair, sloppy pull-over) plays the character as a sleepy, dreamy, emotional invalid. When he first comes on he is accompanying himself, timidly plucking the strings of his fiddle, and at each pluck, timid as it is, he recoils with fright. When he drops his mask he is calmer, inwardly tense; he is always economical in his methods, but at all times his acting has depth, the presence of a strong personality. Unforgettable details: his soundless laugh when Möbius confesses that he has destroyed his notes' (Irma Voser). 'He finishes up in such an abysmal state of resignation that it is he more than any who makes us aware of the melancholy powerlessness of the scientist's existence' (Hans Heinz Holz).

Hans Christian Blech, 'peering up with an alert, covert, mistrustful look, an exaggeratedly ungainly manner – his face possesses a certain worried, introspective quality: his walk is unsteady as if his shambling legs frequently disobeyed him' (Irma Voser). Blech plays the beginning very softly, very compressedly, gathering all his strength for the screaming despair of his *Song of Solomon to be sung to the Cosmonauts*: 'he clings to the table legs like a man who is drunk, then his grin fades, he falls, remains squatting, mummified. When challenged he controls himself and roars farewell in a hard, brutal tone' (Irma Voser).

'In an impossible situation Blech is called upon to create a great love scene from nothing, to reach the highest level of emotion almost from a standing start; as someone who has lost the knack of speaking he must instantly rediscover the power of oratory, he must enact the whole wretchedness of humanity. With his convulsed body, his hard face, his imprisoned view, his sudden blossoming of faith in salvation, his liberated wisdom' (Elisabeth Brock-Sulzer). 'Hanne Hiob's Nurse Monika is sheer shameless devotion, and grasping, impetuous strength; she stands there like a fanatical pioneer on a barricade; her face radiates mirthful joy when he shakes her despairingly. Möbius crumples his handkerchief in his sweating hands, he cowers away from the girl, but then he lures her into the shadows and strangles her' (Irma Voser).

Dürrenmatt wrote the part of the psychiatrist for Therese Giehse. 'When she first comes on, as a hunchbacked old spinster in a white doctor's coat, moving jerkily and disjointedly, with furtive eyes which are either half open or narrowed to invisible slits, an astonished murmur goes through the stalls. In the first Act she is urbane, ebullient, a specialist who inspires trust; she strikes whichever note is right for the people she deals with and in certain circumstances sneers at them behind their backs: to Möbius's ex-wife Frau Rose she displays hearty bonhomie; for Einstein she makes flute-like, gently bewitching sounds; Möbius's "fine boys" arouse studious pathos in her; false, lyrical sweetness is the predominant feature of her attitude to "flourishing life" and yet disdainful, as if she were spitting the words out, of her self-analysis. The first sign she gives of her madness comes when she lets out a little, dry shout, as if she gets carried away by the sound of the name of Solomon' (Irma Voser).

'Her last scene was the most magnificent of all, for at the very moment when she revealed her destructive plans Giehse dared to choose a tone of lyrical ecstasy. When she sang her paean in praise of King Solomon who had chosen her to rule the world, the lovelier and the more enraptured her singing became, the more the audience's horror intensified' (Ivan Nagel). 'Only Newton succumbs to the temptation to burst out laughing. Finally, however, the three physicists cling to each other in mute terror, when the hereditary madness in her stretches and expands, inflates itself to monstrous and horrible proportions, until it breaks out of her in a hysterical fervour of overbearing gestures, and she triumphs as a violent tyrant' (Irma Voser).

THE PHYSICISTS (*London*)

Produced on 9th January 1963 at the Aldwych Theatre, London (Royal Shakespeare Company). Director: Peter Brook; designer: John Bury; translation: James Kirkup. *Fräulein Doktor Mathilde von Zahnd*: Irene Worth; *Möbius*: Cyril Cusack; *Newton*: Michael Hordern; *Einstein*: Alan Webb; *Monika*: Diana Rigg; *Voss*: Clive Swift.

In an interview with Martin Esslin, Dürrenmatt said: '*I had imagined the English actors would underplay much more than the Germans or the Swiss. But not at all. There are some passages where the German casts did more, there are others where the English are far more passionate and emphatic. In one of the best German productions, for example, the mad lady doctor made her revelations at the end sitting quietly on the sofa, using very little voice and emphasis. That gave it a marvellously crazy effect. In Peter Brook's production there is a great deal of movement and vociferation. The London production is also the first I have seen that does not strictly adhere to the set as I described it in the stage directions.*'

Brook's production – set, not in a drawing-room, but in a round room enlivened only by the strong colours of the floor tiles – concentrates on the play less as a discussion of ideas than as a thriller (it reminds even Kenneth Tynan of Hitch-cock). It is 'swift, witty and timed with razor-sharpness' (John Russell Taylor). Brook's tread is sure 'on the tight-ropes he has spun himself, allowing him without flinching to have a vital scene played with the main character seated in a chair placed in the footlights-trough, back to audience' (Bernard Levin). Brook emphasises the funniness of the Secret Agents' feigned madness as a contrast to the incandescent insanity of the Doctor.

'The curtain is up as we enter the theatre, disclosing a spacious, unfriendly room, its wall a continuous curve, its furniture sparse and in some disarray: a table and a standard lamp have been overturned. On the floor there lies a young

woman; . . . undoubtedly dead' (Kenneth Tynan). The merciless treatment of the corpses is contrary to Dürrenmatt's
directions: Brook regards the murders not as mere devices
required by the plot – he unleashes the 'tremendous strength'
referred to by the Police Doctor. The end of the first Act is an
excess: Möbius weeps, Monika screams, defends herself
desperately and is overpowered: 'intellectual *grand-guignol*'
(John Russell Taylor).

For *The Times* critic, the real hall-marks of the production
were the performances Peter Brook had obtained from his
distinguished cast: The main performances are in a manner of
brilliant ambiguity – notably Michael Hordern's mock-
Newton, wig at a drunken angle and alternating between
icily rational courtesy and nervous frenzy. Cyril Cusack,
making a welcome return to London after many years, gives
a nobly subdued account of Möbius. But Irene Worth as the
doctor is the triumph of the production. She shrinks into
the part of the hunchback, creating a whole range of gesture
appropriate to physical disability and which develops from
expressing the authority of reason to the tyranny of madness.
It is a performance worthy to stand beside her Goneril: and
one cannot pay a much higher compliment than that.

THE METEOR (*Zurich, Hamburg, Munich*)

First produced on 20th January 1966 at the Zurich Schau-
spielhaus. Director: Leopold Lindtberg; designer: Teo Otto.
Schwitter: Leonard Steckel; *Muheim*: Gustav Knuth; *Frau
Nomsen*: Mila Kopp.

Produced on 9th February 1966 at the Thalia-Theater,
Hamburg. Director: Hans Lietzau; designer: Jürgen Rose.
Schwitter: O. E. Hasse; *Muheim*: Heinz Klevenow; *Frau
Nomsen*: Heidemarie Hatheyer.

Produced on 12th February 1966 at the Munich Kammerspiele. Director: Hans Schweikart; designer: Jörg Zim-

mermann. *Schwitter*: Paul Verhoeven; *Muheim*: Gerd Brüdern; *Frau Nomsen*: Therese Giehse.

Three settings: Teo Otto's is a decently run-down studio, which could have been used equally well for *La Bohème* or for the first or last Act of Wedekind's *Lulu* (which is also a series of humorous monologues and death scenes); an unspectacularly economical room for an unspectacularly economical production whose intention is simply to back up the play. From Jürgen Rose we get a high cube-shaped room which strains apart the higher it gets until it bursts into a giant crack. On the walls the torn wallpaper hangs down like a luxurious growth and a jungle of painted flesh climbs up to the ceiling. Not any old studio but one which is weird from the first moment, with the sunlight locked out as it tries to get in, bright and harsh, through a window in the back wall. An expressively exaggerated framework for a production which somersaults into the grotesque. Jörg Zimmermann provides a bright attic converted into a studio with an audacious construction of roof beams which almost disappear into the far reaches of the stage, a multifarious arena for a polished psychological interpretation.

Three productions: Leopold Lindtberg, discreet, intent not on creating effects, but on a clear and energetic presentation of the story, consistently brings out the strong appeal of the text, whereby the individuality and strength of the actors have a great deal of scope. Particularly impressive is Gustav Knuth in the rôle of the colossus, Muheim. Because he is so sure of his volume he does not need to roar like a giant, but can express his feelings quite agreeably – the common man with the heart of gold encased in the steely armour of capitalism – and then quarrel earnestly and quite unexaltedly with his fate. It is not his rage that makes him dangerous but the strength with which he controls this rage. His collapse is not sensational; rather he crumbles slowly, almost in slow motion, and precisely because of this, so irresistibly and definitively.

Hans Lietzau, not always very selective in his quest for startling effects and encouraged by the insubstantiality of many of the antagonists, turns the play into a tremendous 'O. E. Hasse Show'. One enthralling moment which catches the mood beautifully is when the Priest enters the pitch-black room and catches sight of Schwitter, lit only by the infernal red glow from the open stove. The fact that the frightened Priest immediately stumbles and knocks over a screen and falls flat on his face; the fact that he hastily gabbles his lines and then, even more exaggeratedly, drops dead; and finally the fact that the four men carrying out the corpse also stumble over the screen and nearly fall – all this means that Lietzau surrenders his one genuine moment of terror to the easy appeal of hammed up macabre tricks.

Hans Schweikart needs half an hour longer than Lindtberg or Lietzau. Convinced that this play, which in itself is so effective, must not be spectacularized like a firework display, he makes the points leisurely and lovingly, one after another. His directorial function extends beyond the script to the actors' unspoken reactions which he handles with equal precision. Schweikart treats the farce seriously: without capers or clowning or showy set pieces, he allows the essential action to unfold, and, contrary, it is true, to Dürrenmatt's intention, he develops individual characters from the sharply outlined farcical types by patient psychological treatment. Over the havoc wrought by Schwitter's frenzied quest for death there falls the ennobling (and also soothing) influence of Wedekind's 'Curse of Absurdity'.

Three Frau Nomsens: to a certain extent Therese Giehse puts her case too well, too penetratingly: she does not come across as a tired old woman already moribund but glad once more to find a listener for her garrulous words of wisdom. Instead she strikes an attitude, delivers a finger-wagging sermon, then dies quite suddenly, almost reluctantly, simply to meet the requirements of the text. Heidemarie Hatheyer, grotesquely deformed and uglified, has other worries: she tortures herself to such an extent in order to force her grand voice into asthmatic wheezing that there is hardly any strength left for the rounding out and shading off of the rôle. The only one of the three who is touching in the rôle of the *terrible lavatory attendant* is Mila Kopp. She simply sits there, speaks in a monotone, with increasingly ponderous pauses, growing visibly exhausted – and by pitiable greatness, pitiable pride alone she achieves the melancholy solitude of dying in harness. *Three Schwitters*: Leonard Steckel (in Dürrenmatt's opinion the ideal casting) is without a doubt the fieriest, the most berserk, and develops the most terrifying vitality in his rage. He is outrageously funny – for instance at the beginning of the second Act when, together with Knuth he juggles with wreaths and rolls them across the stage like car-tyres in a display of mischievous high spirits. Yet he also has moments when his behaviour is ominous and foreboding – for instance, when he dances wildly on the bed, scything the air with wet bandages. O. E. Hasse makes it all more humorous, more sparkling, adding touches of coquetry and just an intriguing hint of playing to the gallery; spiritedly gesticulating, delightedly delivering witty lines and completely imperturbable. He cuts down his closing speech considerably, for despair is alien to his nature – at the very last moment he hurls a stool at the Salvationists in a fit of boyish merriment. Steckel and Hasse: both draw freely on their store of experience, on their extrovert vitality (Steckel's demonic quality definitely creates more excitement) and once they let themselves go, they roar through the reflective, contemplative passages in the text. Paul Verhoeven, a massive, rather dry character actor, who strikes one as being so ungainly and yet displays a surprising agility (therefore, certainly not an 'ideal casting' for this highly emotional rôle), makes a point of using the moments of reflection in order to develop the character: this is most true when he is evincing astonishment at his own liveliness.

Brilliance, hot-headedness, even life-loving irresistibility cannot be wrung from an approach like this; Verhoeven regulates his slightly hoarse voice, which is limited in its range of expression, with such intelligent economy that he seems to gain increasingly in vitality. He acts – in order to make this increase possible – not at full power from start to finish but staggers in literally half-dead at the beginning, to the strains of the funeral march from the Eroica. Then as scene follows scene he grows more and more cheerful, and for one short moment he even enjoys being happy – until he is struck by the crippling realisation that he must live. At the end, his line 'When, oh when will I finally drop dead?' is not thrown aggressively to heaven at the top of his voice, but is said very softly, sadly and despairingly into the silence.

THE METEOR (London)

Produced on 28th July 1966 at the Aldwych Theatre, London (Royal Shakespeare Company). Director: Clifford Williams; designer: John Bury. *Schwitter*: Patrick Magee; *Muheim*: Nicholas Selby; *Frau Nomsen*: Patience Collier.

The Times for 29th July contained the following review by the Drama Critic: 'Like Shaw, Friedrich Dürrenmatt is a writer much preoccupied with artificial morality which, as he presents it, resembles a plywood hut built at the foot of a volcano. In delivering his warning to the hut-dwellers his style has varied between the thriller, the parable, and the complex discussion play which English audiences are inclined to shrug off with the convenient word "Teutonic". They may be relieved to learn that, after the elaboration of *The Physicists*, his new play is a fable rooted in Biblical legend.

'As in his previous fable, *The Visit*, his technique is to take a straightforward situation, change one detail, and observe its calamitous effect on conventional behaviour. The basic situation is the death of a venerated Nobel prize-winning author. Death has been pronounced, commemorative wreaths (one from the National Theatre) have been dispatched, and funeral preparations are under way, but the corpse, ignoring the official evidence, sidles out of the clinic in pyjamas and returns to his old studio.

'Here, with sunlight streaming mercilessly through the windows of John Bury's cavernous set, he spends the rest of the play vainly trying to die – settling into bed in a corpse-like attitude with candles burning at his head, and even imploring his doctor for a lethal injection.

'However, if Schwitter cannot die himself, he is a bringer of death to others. All who come near him either die or lose their reason for living. A clergyman expires on the bed; his young wife commits suicide; his doctor, reputation ruined by his patient's revival, is driven to despair, and a similar fate overtakes his publisher and his former landlord.

'All these characters Schwitter treats with undisguised contempt: but at the end he is visited by an old lavatory attendant procuress – a trader in flesh whom Schwitter, a trader in fantasy, recognises as his equal. Their professions – respectively disreputable and distinguished in the eyes of the world – are both simply unemotional business concerns.

'Dürrenmatt plainly is out to show a good deal more than the spectacle of a state-financed Finnegan's Wake: and, indeed, where he does exploit this aspect of the situation – with a ridiculous parson and a ludicrous critic – the comedy declines from the grotesque to the stereotyped. But it is nevertheless on this commonplace level that the fable makes most sense. Elsewhere the governing idea of the play is that death, 'the only reality', is an intolerable companion to the living as it exposes the futility of all human aspiration.

'Even if one accepts this (which I do not), it hardly explains the death of Schwitter's victims. They die from a variety of causes, but not from an encounter with a desolating truth.

The fable drives through energetically enough, but it is a blunt instrument. And accepting Schwitter himself as a counter-Lazarus figure, there is as much sentimentality as irony in his agonised last moments, surrounded by a Salvation Army band and still not dead.

'Patrick Magee plays him with plentiful use of his famous sardonic croak, and scoring up reliable comedy from the spectacle of unquenchable vitality inside a shroud. There are two superb smaller performances by Robert Eddison as the doctor, examining his patient in a style of murderous assault, and Patience Collier as the old bawd: a pitiably dilapidated figure, firmly steeled against emotion, pity most of all.'

PLAY STRINDBERG (*Newcastle*)

Produced on 14th January 1972 at the University Theatre, Newcastle. *Kurt*: Freddie Jones; *Alice*: Yvonne Mitchell; *Edgar*: Gerald Flood.

Sid Chaplin wrote in *The Guardian*: Of pyhsical violence there is none for none is needed. Verbal assault does better and is quicker. The fight launches itself out of boredom and is kept going by a competitive hatred so fertile in invention that if it could be put to use, it would surely transform the desert into a green wonder. As in real life, comedy quickens and holds together moments of pure farce often dangerously on the brink of the farcical.

These were the moments when I trembled and they often followed the loudest laughs of the night. In retrospect, I can now count these as among the best moments I have ever had in the theatre. That the play has these tremendous moments (quite apart from the flow of interest securely based on self-identification) is due primarily to the magnificent teamwork and discipline of the players – Miss Yvonne Mitchell as the wife, Mr Freddie Jones in the opposing rôle, and Mr Gerald Flood as the lover who is forced to referee. They act all the time in concert. Discipline paid off and what must have been an ordeal in rehearsal became a triumph.

If I particularly mention Miss Mitchell it is not to make odious comparisons but to remark on a triumph which is essentially Strindberg's. In every way she is the woman he created and for whom Dürrenmatt has now provided the perfect vehicle – a bane and a bitter-sweet curse, an incubus kittenish and callous in turn but in spite of this a woman in every way desirable. It will be long before I forget her.

THE CONFORMER (*Sheffield*)

Produced on 23rd January 1975 in the Sheffield Crucible Studio. Director: Ian Giles; designer: Richard Brown. *Doc*: David Howey; *Boss*: Bill Wallis; *Cop*: David Leland.

Robin Thornber wrote in *The Guardian*: Where Brecht made his parodies of American gangsterism the logical development of capitalism, Dürrenmatt corkscrews his way through the machinations of a Keystone Cops assassination racket to the point where anarchism and anarchy come together in the sensual inevitability of killing. Doc is dissolving corpses in his grisly basement brewery because society has trampled on his good intentions. His son wants to use wealth and crime to purge a corrupt society (and if society is not corrupt, why do all these clergymen keep falling down the steps of brothels?)

The son, believe it or not, ends up in the vats and the district attorney takes over the organisation. Ian Giles's production gives the gruesome farce the edge of hysteria it needs to carry its points home. Bill Wallis as the boss, parodies every Hollywood gangster you've ever seen until you believe in them all; David Leland is the corrupt Colombo cop with a chip on his shoulder that goes right through his brain; and David Howey is the innocent who disposes of the evidence. There are, in case you're nervous, shocks in the language, in a naked body, and in some very loud bangs. But if that is going to upset you, you will find the play's implications unbearable.

Bibliography

WORKS BY DÜRRENMATT

1 *Stage Plays*

(a) In German (all published by Verlag der Arche, Zurich, except where stated otherwise)

Es steht geschrieben. Basle 1947 (Sammlung Klosterberg. Schweizerische Reihe); Zurich 1959

Der Blinde. Berlin 1947; Zurich 1960. (Printed version.)

Der Turmbau von Babel. 1949. (Destroyed.)

Romulus der Große. Printed version, Basle 1956; 2nd version 1957, Zurich 1958; 3rd version 1961; 4th version 1964.

Die Ehe des Herrn Mississippi. Zurich 1952; 2nd version 1957; 3rd version 1964; film version 1961. Also: 'Drehbuch des Autors', 1961 (appeared with the stage version 1966).

Ein Engel kommt nach Babylon. Zurich 1954; 2nd version 1958.

Der Besuch der alten Dame. (Original title: *Komödie der Hochkonjunktur*.) Zurich 1956; film version 1963.

Frank der Fünfte: Oper einer Privatbank. (Music by Paul Burkhard.) 1959; Zurich 1960.

Die Physiker. Zurich 1962. (TV version 1963.)

Herkules und der Stall des Augias. Zurich 1960 (Die kleinen Bücher der Arche 283/4); New edition, Zurich 1963. (On record, DGG No. 43013 1957.)

Der Meteor. Zurich 1966. (Also in TV version.)

Die Wiedertäufer. Zurich 1967.

König Johann. Nach Shakespeare. Zurich 1968.

Play Strindberg. 1969. (Nach Strindbergs Trauerspiel *Totentanz*.)

Porträt eines Planeten. Zurich 1970. (Düsseldorf version. 1970; Zurich version. 1971.)

Urfaust 1970. (Bearbeitung des Goetheschen Werkes.)

Titus Andronicus. Eine Komödie nach Shakespeare. Zurich 1970.

Der Mitmacher. 1973. Printed version, Zurich 1976.

Komödien I comprising *Romulus Mississippi, Engel,* all in second versions, and *Besuch der alten Dame).* 1957.

Komödien II und frühe Stücke (comprising *Es steht geschrieben, Der Blinde, Frank der Fünfte, Die Physiker* and *Herkules).* 1964.

Komödien III (comprising *König Johann, Der Meteor, Play Strindberg, Titus* and *Die Wiedertäufer).* 1972
Die Frist, Zurich 1977.

(b) In School Editions

Der Besuch der alten Dame. Ed. P. K. Ackermann. London: Methuen 1961.

Romulus der Grosse. Ed. H. F. Garten. London: Methuen 1962.

Die Physiker. Ed. A. Taylor. London: Macmillan 1966.

(c) In English translation

The Visit. London: Cape 1962 and 1973.

Four Plays 1957–1962 (comprising *Romulus the Great, The Marriage of Mr Mississippi, An Angel Comes to Babylon* and *The Physicists).* London: Cape 1964.

The Meteor. London: Cape 1973.

Play Strindberg. London: Cape 1973.

2 Radio Plays

(a) In German

Gesammelte Hörspiele (comprising *Abendstunde im Spätherbst, Der Doppelgänger, Herkules und der Stall des Augias, Nächtliches Gespräch mit einem verachteten Menschen, Die Panne, Der Prozess um des Esels Schatten, Stranitzky und der Nationalheld, Das Unternehmen der Wega,* all of which have also been published separately). Zurich: Arche 1961.

(b) In English translation

Incident at Twilight (Abendstunde im Spätherbst) in *Postwar German Theatre,* eds. M. Benedikt and G. E. Wellwarth. London: Macmillan 1968.

3 *Novels*

(a) In German

Der Richter und sein Henker. Einsiedeln: Benziger 1952; 2nd edition 1957; Reinbek: Rowohlt 1955 (rororo-Taschenbuch No. 150).

Der Verdacht. Einsiedeln: Benziger 1953; Reinbek: Rowohlt 1961 (rororo-Taschenbuch No. 448).

Grieche sucht Griechin. Zurich: Arche 1955; Frankfurt: Ullstein 1958 (Ullstein Bücher No. 199).

Das Versprechen. Zurich: Arche 1958 (From the script to Dürrenmatt's film 'Es geschah am hellichten Tag').

Der Sturz. Zurich: Arche 1971.

(b) In School Editions

Der Richter und sein Henker. Ed. L. Forster. London: Harrap 1962.

Der Verdacht. Ed. L. Forster. London: Harrap 1965.

Das Versprechen. Ed. L. Forster. London: Harrap 1967.

(c) In English translation

The Judge and his Hangman. London: Jenkins 1954; London: Cape 1967; London: Penguin 1969.

The Pledge. London: Cape 1959; London: Penguin 1964.

The Quarry (*Der Verdacht*). London: Cape 1962.

Once a Greek (*Grieche sucht Griechin*). London: Cape 1966.

4 *Short stories and prose pieces*

(a) In German

Die Stadt: Prosa I–IV (comprising *Weihnacht, Der Folterknecht, Der Hund, Das Bild des Sisyphos, Der Theaterdirektor, Die Falle, Die Stadt, Der Tunnel, Pilatus*). Zurich: Arche 1952.

Die Panne. Zurich: Arche 1956.

(b) In School Editions

Die Panne and Der Tunnel. Ed. F. J. Alexander. London: Oxford University Press 1967.

(c) In English translation

A Dangerous Game (*Die Panne*). London: Cape 1960.

The Tunnel in *Modern German Stories*. Ed. H. M. Waidson. London: Faber 1961.

The Tunnel in *Deutsche Reihe für Ausländer*, Reihe F, vol III. Munich: Hueber 1964.

5 *Essays and speeches*

(a) In German

Theater-Schriften und Reden (containing most of his pre-1965 theoretical and critical utterances). Zurich: Arche 1966.

Tschechoslowakei 1968 (Speeches held on 8 September 1968 by Dürrenmatt, Frisch, Bichsel, Grass and Kurt Marti in the Stadttheater Basle). Zurich 1968.

Monstervortrag über Gerechtigkeit und Recht. Zurich 1969.

Sätze aus Amerika. Zurich 1970.

Dramaturgisches und Kritisches (*Theater-Schriften und Reden* Vol. II). Zurich: Arche 1972.

Zusammenhänge. Essay über Israel. Zurich 1976.

(b) In English translation

Problems of the Theatre (*Theaterprobleme*) in *Tulane Drama Review*, III, i (Oct. 1958), pp. 3–26; also in *Four Plays 1957–62* (see above); and elsewhere.

Writings on Theatre and Drama. London: Cape 1976.

6 *Miscellaneous*

Die Heimat im Plakat (scurrilous sketches). Zurich: Diogenes 1963.

INTERVIEWS WITH DÜRRENMATT

(a) In German

Egon Vietta (ed.): *Theater–Darmstädter Gespräch*. Darmstadt 1955.

Ernst Schumacher: 'Interview mit Friedrich Dürrenmatt'. *Deutsche Woche* (Munich), 18 January 1961.

Horst Bienek: 'Werkstattgespräch mit Friedrich Dürrenmatt', in *Werkstattgespräche mit Schriftsellern*. Munich: Hanser 1962.

Siegfried Melchinger: 'Friedrich Dürrenmatt–Theater ist Theater'. *Theater Heute*, September, *1968*, *pp.* 6–8; also in *Theater im Umbruch*, ed. H. Rischbieter. Munich: DTV 1970.

Artur Joseph: '. . . weshalb man ein Drama schreibt'. Süddeutsche Zeitung 6/9.2. 1969.

(b) In English

'Dürrenmatt Discusses His Latest Play (The Physicists)', *The Times*, 5 January 1963.

Martin Esslin: 'Merciless Observer', *Plays and Players*, X, vi (March 1963), pp. 15–16.

Horst Bienek: 'Friedrich Dürrenmatt' in *The Playwright Speaks*, ed. Walter Wager, London: Longmans 1969.

Violet Ketels: 'Friedrich Dürrenmatt at Temple University': Journal of Modern Languages I, 1971 pp. 68–108.

Kenneth S. Whitton: 'Afternoon conversation with an uncomfortable person', in *New German Studies*, 2, 1974, pp. 14–30 (Interview in Neuchâtel 1969).

WRITINGS ON DÜRRENMATT

1 *Monographs*

(a) In German

Arnold, Armin: *Friedrich Dürrenmatt*. Berlin 1969; 3rd enlarged edn. 1974.

Banziger, Hans: *Frisch und Dürrenmatt*. Bern: Francke, 1960; 6th edn. 1971.

Brock-Sulzer, Elisabeth: *Friedrich Dürrenmatt, Stationen seines Werkes*. Zurich: Arche 1960; 4th edn. 1973.

Brock-Sulzer, Elisabeth: *Dürrenmatt in unserer Zeit*. Basle 1968; 2nd edn. 1971.

Durzak, Manfred: *Dürrenmatt, Frisch, Weiss*. Stuttgart 1972.

Jäggi, Willy (ed.): *Der unbequeme Dürrenmatt* (6 essays by Elisabeth Brock-Sulzer, Fritz Buri, Reinhold Grimm, Hans Mayer, Werner Oberle, and Gottfried Benn), vol. 4 in the series 'Theater unserer Zeit'. Basle: Basilius 1962.

Jauslin, Christian: *Friedrich Dürrenmatt, Zur Struktur seiner Dramen*. Zurich: Juris 1965.

Knapp, Gerhard P.: *Friedrich Dürrenmatt: Studien zu seinem Werk*. Heidelberg 1975.

Mayer, Hans: *Dürrenmatt und Frisch, Anmerkungen*, vol. 4 in the series 'Opuscula aus Wissenschaft und Dichtung'. Pfullingen: Neske 1963.

Neumann, Gerhard (ed.): *Dürrenmatt Frisch Weiss*. Munich 1969.

Profitlich, Ulrich: *Friedrich Dürrenmatt, Komödienbegriff und Komödienstruktur*. Stuttgart 1973.

Spycher, Peter: *Friedrich Dürrenmatt. Das erzählerische Werk*. Stuttgart 1972

Text + Kritik: *Friedrich Dürrenmatt I* (No. 50/51). Munich 1976.

(b) in English

Arnold, Armin: *Friedrich Dürrenmatt*. New York 1972.

Peppard, Murray B.: *Friedrich Dürrenmatt*, no. 87 in Twayne's World Authors Series'. New York: Twayne 1969.

2 *Articles in Periodicals and Books,*
and Sections of Larger Works

(a) In German

ALLEMANN, Beda: 'Die Struktur der Komödie bei Frisch und Dürrenmatt', in *Das deutsche Lustspiel* 1969, pp. 200–219.

BERGHAHN, Wilfried: 'Friedrich Dürrenmatts Spiel mit den Ideologien', *Frankfurter Hefte* XI, ii (1956), p. 100 ff.

KUCZYNSKI, Jürgen: 'Friedrich Dürrenmatt – Humanist', *Neue Deutsche Literatur* 12, 1964. No. 8, pp. 59–90; No. 9, pp. 35–55.

KUHNE, Erich: 'Satire und groteske Dramatik', *Weimarer Beiträge*, 12 Jg., 1966, pp. 539–65.

MADLER, Herbert: 'Dürrenmatts mutiger Mensch', *Hochlan* 62, 1970, pp. 36–49.

POSER, Therese: 'Friedrich Dürrenmatt' (dealing with *Romulus* and *Engel*) in Rolf Geissler (ed.), *Zur Interpretation des modernen Dramas*. Frankfurt: Diesterweg 1960, p. 69ff.

Strelka, Joseph: Brecht, Horvath, Dürrenmatt, Wege und Abwege des modernen Dramas. Vienna: Forum 1962.

(b) In English

ASKEW, Melvin W.: 'Dürrenmatt's *The Visit of the Old Lady*', *Tulane Drama Review*, V, iv (June 1961), pp. 89–105.

DAVIAU, Donald G.: 'Justice in the works of Friedrich Dürrenmatt', *Kentucky Foreign Language Quarterly*, IX, iv (1962), p. 181ff.

DAVIAU, Donald G.: 'The Role of "Zufall" in the writings of Friedrich Dürrenmatt', *Germanic Review*, 47, 1972, pp. 281–93.

DILLER, Edward: 'Friedrich Dürrenmatt's Theological Concept of History', *German Quarterly*, XL, iii (1967), pp. 363–71.

DILLER, Edward: 'Aesthetics and the Grotesque: Friedrich Dürrenmatt', *Wisconsin Studies in Contemporary Literature*, VII (1966), pp. 328–35.

DILLER, Edward: 'Despair and the Paradox: Friedrich Dürrenmatt', *Drama Survey*, V, ii (1966), pp. 131–6.

DILLER, Edward: 'Dürrenmatt's Use of the Stage as a Dramatic Element', *Symposium*, XX, iii (1966), pp. 197–206.

DILLER, Edward: 'Human Dignity in a Materialistic Society: Friedrich Dürrenmatt and Bertolt Brecht', *Modern Language Quarterly*, XXV, iv (1964), pp. 451–60.

GONTRUM, Peter B.: 'Ritter, Tod und Teufel: Protagonists and Antagonists in the Prose Works of Friedrich Dürrenmatt', *Seminar*, I (1965), p. 88ff.

GUTH, Hans P.: 'Dürrenmatt's *Visit*: The Play behind the Play', *Symposium*, XVI (Summer 1962), pp. 94–102.

HANSEL, J: 'Friedrich Dürrenmatt – Bibliographie'. Verlag Gehlen, 1968.

HEILMAN, Robert B.: 'Tragic Elements in a Dürrenmatt Comedy', *Modern Drama*, X, i (1967), pp. 11–16.

HOLZAPFEL, Robert: 'The Divine Plan Behind the Plays of Friedrich Dürrenmatt', *Modern Drama*, VIII, iii (1965), pp. 237–46.

HORTENBACH, Jenny C.: 'Biblical Echoes in Dürrenmatt's *Der Besuch der alten Dame*', *Monatshefte*, LVII, iv (1965), pp. 145–61.

JONAS, K. W.: 'Die Dürrenmatt-Literatur', *Börsenblatt für den deutschen Buchhandel*, Frankfurter Ausgabe 24 Jg, 23.7.68, pp. 1725–1736, (1947–1967).

KLARMANN, Adolf: 'Friedrich Dürrenmatt and the Tragic Sense of Comedy', *Tulane Drama Review*, IV, iv (1960), pp. 77–104; also in: T. Bogard and W. I. Oliver (eds.), *Modern Drama*, New York: Oxford U. P., 1965, p. 99ff.

LORAM, Ian C.: '*Der Besuch der alten Dame* and *The Visit*', *Monatshefte*, LIII, i (1961), pp. 15–21.

PEPPARD, Murray B.: 'The Grotesque in Dürrenmatt's Drama', *Kentucky Foreign Language Quarterly*, IX, i (1962), pp. 36–44.

PFEIFFER, John: 'Windows, detectives and justice in Dürrenmatt's detective stories', *Revue des Langues Vivantes*, 33, 1967, pp. 451–460.

REED, Eugene E.: Dürrenmatt's *Der Besuch der alten Dame*: a study in the Grotesque', *Monatshefte*, LIII, i (1961), pp. 9–14.

REED, Eugene E.: 'The Image of the Unimaginable: A Note on Dürrenmatt's *Der Richter und sein Henker*', *Revue des Langues Vivantes*, XXVII, ii (1961), pp. 117–23.

SHEPPARD, Vera: 'Friedrich Dürrenmatt as a Dramatic Theorist', *Drama Survey*, IV, iii, (1965), pp. 244–63.

USMIANI, Renate: 'Friedrich Dürrenmatt as Wolfgang Schwitter: An Autobiographical Interpretation of *The Meteor*', *Modern Dramas*, XI, ii (1968), pp. 143–50.

USMIANI, Renate: 'Friedrich Dürrenmatt, escape artist. A look at the novels', *Mosaic*, 5, 1971/72, pp. 27–41.

USMIANI, Renate: 'Masterpiece in disguise. The radio plays of Friedrich Dürrenmatt', *Seminar*, 7, 1971, pp. 42–57.

WAIDSON, H. M.: 'Friedrich Dürrenmatt' in: Alex Natan (ed.), *German Men of Letters* vol. 3, London: Wolff 1964; revised and expanded in: Alex Natan (ed.), *Swiss Men of Letters*, London: Wolff 1970.

WEIMAR, Karl S.: 'The Scientist and Society: A Study of Three Modern Plays', *Modern Language Quarterly*, XXVII, iv (1966), pp. 431–48.

WELLWARTH, George E.: 'Friedrich Dürrenmatt and Max Frisch: Two Views of the Drama', *Tulane Drama Review*, VI, iii (1962), pp. 14–42.

WHITTON, Kenneth S.: 'The Zürcher Literaturstreit', *German Life and Letters*, xxvii, No. 2, 1974, pp. 142–50.

WHITTON, Kenneth S.: 'Friedrich Dürrenmatt and the legacy of Bertolt Brecht', *Forum for Modern Language Studies*, xii, No. 1, 1976, pp. 65–81.

Index